Corners Untouched by Madness

Based on a true story

Between the Lines Publishing, LLC

Published by Between the Lines Publishing, LLC (USA) Liminal Books
(imprint)
410 Caribou Trail, Lutsen, Minnesota 55612, USA

www.btwnthelines.com

Cover artist: Suzanne Johnson

Contributing Editor: Polly Tuckett

Corners Untouched by Madness
N. Daniel

Paperback ISBN: 978-1-950502-12-7
Hardcover ISBN: 978-1-950502-13-4

Also Available in Ebook format

"This is my love letter to all of the people that I have hurt. This is a story about trying to be better. I want to show you that exposing our sins is the only way that we can ever heal. These are all the mistakes I have committed that I would not want a stranger to know about me. I would lay down my armor, my safety, my reputation, my honor to ensure that even the most powerless among you has a voice. I would dig down to my lowest point if only to raise you up once again."

- N. Daniel

For Elliot

Part One

Daniel

1

In a small stucco house in rural Mexico a man lay dying. Past a crooked doorframe and through an overgrown yard someone was moving, the knife in his hand thrown in a shadow on the wall. Broken furniture lay strewn across the space. A patch of crimson blotted the floor. Dark shapes moved from room to room. A shrill repeated cry – "Verdad!"

I awoke disorientated and clammy, beads of sweat on my forehead. 'Verdad' – what did it mean? The nightmares had returned. It was a hot summer night and I was tangled in my sheets. As usual I was only wearing one sock, having kicked the other off in my sleep. "Verdad." Maybe I had picked it up somewhere in my high school Spanish class. The clock read 4:14 a.m. in red glowing numerals and I felt a dull sense of dread with the knowledge that I had to get out of bed in a few short hours. I closed my eyes.

In the morning, I looked at myself for a long while in the bathroom mirror. My blue eyes seemed cloudy and a five o'clock shadow stretched across my face. I decided not to shave. The hair on my face balanced the fuzz on my shaved head. Walking into the bedroom I pulled on some jeans and a Mexican National Team jersey.

I poured myself some cereal and sat down at the table, switching on my laptop. I quickly glanced at what was going on in the US, then

1

switched over to the Latin American page. I used to be a drug user, and now, clean and sober, I felt a moral responsibility to keep up with the forgotten war raging at our doorstep. Although I wasn't Mexican, the influence of their struggle had impacted my life in ways that felt very personal and I was looking for signs of hope. Today was like so many others, a horror show; news about mass graves and bodies piling up. I felt sick and helpless but still I carried on eating my cereal.

Gradually I moved on to the rest of the world, to areas like the Middle East, North Korea, Tibet, and Sudan. All the places where conflict and tragedy seemed to reign supreme. I was looking for gems, stories of courage, proof that things were improving. All I found was hurt.

I put the empty cereal bowl in the sink. My cat ran the length of his body against my calves and I looked down at his bowl. I poured in some kibble, wondering how he could tolerate the stuff day in and day out. He seemed content, and I didn't mind him, though I would have much rather been living with a woman. The cat didn't require much maintenance so, for now, he won.

I pulled a big stainless-steel kettle full of soup out of the fridge. I loved cooking projects and had challenged myself to cook a different kind of soup every week for five months. Today it was fruit and nut chili and next week it would be chicken corn chowder. I spooned out some chili into a plastic container and tightly popped a lid on. Leaving the apartment, I tried my best not to get the cat's head caught in the door.

I reached the office early and pulled out my keycard to open the thick glass door. My company was in a large, concrete industrial complex that housed several other businesses. I walked by a large metallic sign that read "Lacroix Corporation" and passed a display case housing several oversized replica championship rings. The company had been around for over a century and lauded themselves for their ability to craft fine jewelry for overpaid professional athletes.

When I was hired my grandmother had given me her class ring which was made by Lacroix. It was small and simple with a large stylized "GC" on the top and the numbers nineteen and forty-four written on either side. The initials stood for Grace City, North Dakota – a small farming village in the center of the state. Only two of the rings had been made, one for her and the other for my grandfather's brother, the only members of her graduating class. I wore it around my neck on a chain, a reminder that this was where I was meant to be. It was an honor and I often showed it to others. I wondered if its complement still existed, maybe in an old shoebox gathering dust in a relative's attic.

In the cafeteria there was no one to be seen. I placed my soup in a giant refrigerator. Two of the senior artists entered the room, chatting.

"I can't believe they are shifting some of our workload over to cheaper designers in the Dominican Republic," one said. "I wonder if it is going to be like Mexico all over again."

Mexico? I stopped dead in my tracks. A chill shot down my spine. I heard that the company had once had an agreement to send aspects of its production across the border, though I didn't know the specifics. Apparently, it had backfired and was bad for Lacroix financially. I walked past the men. My legs seemed fragile, my steps light.

"Well, this is a little different. There are no shipments of gold to worry about. I just hope the Dominicans do a good job and don't make us look bad."

"Yeah," the first man replied. "I am just afraid we will lose our asses again."

I wondered if Lacroix's brief stint in Mexico had anything to do with the night before. Perhaps it was a mystical sign for us to help. I suppose I was the only one listening out for something like that, a pattern in the coincidences of daily life. I just wasn't sure what to do about it.

Exiting the cafeteria, I took a sharp left turn, walking through a long corridor between cubicles. It was seldom filled with friendly faces and, on bad days, the place was an icy gauntlet. I made my way to my cubicle, lost in a far corner that you actually had to be going to specifically to find.

I sat down at my desk and turned on my computer. While it booted up, I felt a shot of pain in my neck and fingers and a thrill of loneliness anticipating the hours spent in isolation. My coworkers were always hard at work and sat there with music blasting in their ears, heads buried in stacks of paper or staring dumbly at a screen. When I wasn't attempting conversation, a deafening silence fell over the office that seemed to lend a rhythm to the creaks in my vertebrae. My attempts at humor fell flat, and there always seemed to be cool air hanging in the cubicle afterward. Conditions like these crushed a person's will, extinguishing any spark of originality. I checked my messages and then headed to the filing cabinets. There was a lot of work to do today.

Daniel

2

I worked a little later than usual, leaving the office around 6:00 p.m. We were behind schedule, and I had been placed in a position where I could gain ground for the company. I often had to make sacrifices in order to keep our projects running on time, but I didn't mind. Lacroix Corporation had a good reputation and that reflected well upon me.

I exited the parking lot and merged onto the freeway. Tonight, I was going to see Levi, an old friend. We were operating a small self-publishing company. Our business was still in its infancy and we were struggling to find clients. Recently we had gotten a few bites and were both anxious to get on with our first big project. When we weren't churning out ideas for the business we would reminisce about our times in middle and high school together.

I sped through the highways of Minneapolis losing myself in the familiar landmarks along the way. When I reached Levi's small house in Saint Paul, his wife Anna greeted me at the door. She had also been with us since middle school. She looked like Tinkerbell with her dark, pixie haircut. Her three small lost boys sat at the dinner table. I laughed as they tried to cram pieces of food into their mouths while most wound up on the floor. Anna called Levi and a few moments later he appeared from the kitchen. The kids left the table in a maelstrom of excitement, grabbing his legs so he could drag their bodies across the floor as he waded over to greet me.

"Good to see you again, Daniel. What have you been up to lately?"

"Just slaving away behind my desk. How about you?"

"Oh, you know. Trying to run a publishing company with no money."

"Hah," was all I could muster. It was too true to be funny.

He smiled and offered me a seat in the living room. Pulling out a business style binder with our notes, he eagerly discussed current projects and marketing strategies. We had been working on a coffee-table book about celebrity impersonators for the past month or two and seemed to finally be making headway. Levi was editing and I was designing. The author was having trouble getting organized. Anna brought in some strong coffee and the subject changed to planning a business trip to Detroit, linked to a book by one of our prospective authors.

This project seemed daunting. Recently several photographers had made books about Detroit's decline, popularly dubbed "disaster porn". We had contacted a photojournalist in the city who had an idea. Why not make a book on the city's regeneration? It was a good opportunity and we both jumped at the chance. This book was a work in progress, and we were excited at the prospect of a fresh adventure.

When the brainstorming session was over Levi and I retired to the basement where he showed me some catalogs of masonry equipment he had been photographing. I briefly thumbed through them, each page looking like the next. Our conversation bounced back and forth between business, stories of our youthful days clowning around in school and the romance which was relentlessly carving a place in my heart.

"Do you remember Mei?" I asked.

Levi looked up from the musty pages.

"Yeah, didn't she graduate from Harvard or Yale or something? It's funny, but Anna actually used to help her with her math homework."

I found this amusing because Mei was somewhat of a genius in my eyes. I gathered the courage to speak a little more on the topic.

"I've been talking to her a bit on social media. It's kind of embarrassing, but I sort of have a crush on her."

Levi fell silent. We both knew that she was out of my league. I had no idea why she would even talk to me, but I loved every minute of it. He licked his thumb and went ahead several pages in the catalog. I became nervous, suddenly fearful that Levi would squash my hopes of ever being with her.

"You know she lives halfway across the country, right?"

"Mere details," I brushed off the question.

Just then a voice echoed down the long basement corridor.

"Levi?" It was Anna. "Can you come up here and put the kids to bed?"

"Duty calls," he sighed, rising from his chair.

"I guess this is my cue to leave," I said, standing up and offering Levi a firm handshake. He now knew about my feelings for Mei and hadn't necessarily dismissed them. It emboldened me.

"Same time next week?"

"You bet," I replied.

As I navigated my way home through the darkened streets I could think only of Mei. I hadn't ever really known her in school. Shy, quiet and extremely brilliant, she was in a class of her own. With raven hair, caramel skin, a round face and wire-rim glasses, she was the quintessential brainiac. From those innocent days she had grown into a beautiful woman with a mind as sharp as an acute angle. She made me feel like I was someone valuable. To most women I wasn't worth the honesty of a rejection. They just ignored me. I was dying for Mei, but the fact that she lived in Baltimore was something of a problem. On lonely nights spent whittling away in my apartment I longed to know what she smelled like, what she tasted like, how her skin would feel against mine. It would have been heaven. I feared she would always remain an intangible muse, an archetype for the perfect female and, I suppose, to others, this would seem blown completely out of proportion. She was human after all, but the ideal of Mei was irresistible to me.

In high school I was no one, just a pot-smoking art student who had no reservations about making a complete ass of himself. Someone like Mei had no reason to talk to me and vice versa. When I did see her in the hallway, she was usually carrying her books and smiling with her friends. I was like a little kid with no money and his face pressed up against a warmly lit shop window. She was so desirable. Even if I had realized it back then, I still couldn't compete with the other males in our class. So, I eventually gave up, taking harder drugs and letting my addictions lead me into an accidental overdose. I hit rock bottom. Piece by piece I rebuilt my life in an image more like hers. I got clean, went to college and graduated with distinction. Suddenly she had reappeared in my life, though up until now I seldom spoke of her. Who was she, really, and why had she made this entrance?

It started raining a little and the pavement glistened. I looked down at my ragged tennis shoes splashing through the puddles. I was home late. My cat was there to greet me at the door, and I paused by the cutting board on my kitchen counter. Placing my hands on the edge I stared into the woodgrain. I could feel her arms around me. It was love. It was hurt. It felt real but I was all alone. I reveled in the stillness and knew I was powerless. Pursuing her felt criminal. To catch her would be like capturing a butterfly, putting it in a jar and screwing down the lid. It wouldn't survive for long. All I could do was stand there in silence, tracing the whorls in the wood, trapped by a figment of my imagination. Was she thinking of me too? Her virtual presence remained for several more sensual moments before fading into the small fissures that had formed around the edges of the board.

Walking into the bathroom I returned to the mirror and stared hard at my lanky frame. In the corner of my eye I caught a flash of a dark image lurking behind me. Startled, I shook my head and rubbed my eyes with my open palms. Was my mind playing tricks on me? I groaned.

"What the hell is wrong with you?" I wondered aloud. For some reason I felt as though I would never really know. I pulled some pills out from behind my reflection and swallowed them down. Burrowing under the covers, sleep came quickly.

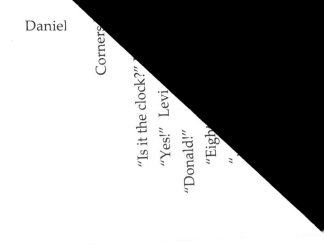

Daniel

"Corners"

"Is it the clock?"

"Yes!" Levi

"Donald!"

"Eigh

3

Before our trip to Detroit, I purchased two baseball caps: a Detroit Lions hat for Levi and a Michigan Wolverines hat for myself. I figured that if we were going to an unfamiliar city, appeasing the locals with sports diplomacy was key to our success. We packed into the car in the evening and drove the kids to Levi's parents' house near Winona, Minnesota. The kids slept for most of the trip, and when they woke up, we threw french fries at them as they tried to catch and eat them.

"Okay, kids," Levi commanded. "Who wants to play a game?"

The kids returned, "Me, me!" in unison.

"So, let's play I spy!"

The kids looked confused. Julian, the oldest, spoke up.

"Dad, it's dark outside! What are we supposed to find?"

Levi rubbed his chin.

"I spy something bright."

"Car light?" Donald, the middle child asked.

"Which car light?" Levi replied.

The youngest child pointed toward the dashboard.

"What do you see, Edward?"

Apparently, he could not immediately put words to his thought. He was only three years old.

Julian asked.

exclaimed. "...And what time is it?" he paused.

t o'clock," Julian replied, out of turn.

...And what does that mean?"

The kids groaned.

"Bedtime," Julian frowned.

"That's right. Now, Daniel has promised to give the first one to fall asleep five dollars."

I gave Levi a dirty look and he winked at me. The kids bodies went limp and they feigned snoring. After ten minutes they really did fall asleep. I took three five dollar bills out of my wallet and placed them on the center armrest.

"You don't have to do that, Daniel. They will forget as soon as they wake up."

"Julian won't forget. Besides, when am I going to have cash again? I only withdraw it when I go on road trips. Might as well put it to good use," I reminded him.

"Are you telling me you know my kids better than I do?"

"Not what I said," I argued.

"Fair enough then."

We arrived on the outskirts of Winona twenty minutes later. The kids were happy to see their grandparents when we dropped them at the isolated farmhouse, but with their absence came the thought that Levi was taking a big risk on their future by pouring money into our company. Were we doing the right thing? We drove on through the night, past Madison and Chicago, taking turns along the way.

I felt a special kinship with the idea of Detroit. The city's mottos, "Speramus Meliora" and "Resurget Cineribus" or "We hope for better things" and "It will rise from the ashes", were adopted after the great fire of 1805. These days very few people dared to enter the city with hopes of promoting new growth, and even fewer succeeded.

Levi and I pulled into a roadside oasis. We got out of the car and stretched our legs. I bought coffee and string cheese and returned to the car where Levi was placing the gas pump back in its holster. I gave him a cup of coffee in exchange for the receipt, placing the slip of paper behind the rearview mirror.

"How are our finances?" he asked.

At the time we were experiencing one of the worst economic recessions in the history of the United States. Levi had a family and me, just a wild glint in my eye and a desire to improve the world. We could be the duo that would make a difference for the country! Who else was going to achieve this goal if not us? I imagined Levi and I in the back seat of a convertible during a ticker-tape parade, marching through the streets of downtown Detroit. *No, that can't be right*, I thought to myself. I rubbed the bridge of my nose with my thumb and index finger and squeezed my eyes shut.

"We'll get this book on Detroit made," I finally replied, afraid I might still be sugar coating things.

"You do understand I abandoned my family to do this with you, right?"

I winced.

"I have a cat you know. Don't think I have nothing riding on this. Thanks to your wife for checking in on him by the way."

Levi shook his head and let out a small chuckle.

"Daniel, you need your own wife. Then you would know how much this could mean."

"Let's make lots of money when we get there. That will make your wife happy."

As we drove, our conversation ebbed and flowed in the darkness with a singular focus that the headlights seemed to illuminate. There was hope, a great hope, that what we were doing could be helpful to people. We knew what we were doing was small scale, but to us driving six hundred miles across country was a big deal. Yes, we were entrepreneurs trying to make a profit, but this was our kind of project and we were seriously digging it.

We pulled into Detroit mid-morning and met Ben, our contact, at a locally owned coffee shop. It was on a small, quiet street bordering the massive skyscrapers and the aging houses of residential Detroit. The place was bustling with people; we had been expecting the odd mirage in a concrete desert, but here were pockets of activity fizzing with life. The people were friendly and hospitable. Like us, they were independent businesspeople with an iron will to survive, to grow and prosper.

Ben was a freelance photojournalist who had worked for many big-name publications. He had a passion for the city. With his talent he could have worked anywhere in the world, but his love for Detroit kept him close to the city. This relayed an extraordinary sense of honesty. Why couldn't the rest of the country see Detroit with Ben's point of view?

Once a thriving metropolis, Detroit was now a ghost town, with whole districts abandoned. Most of the population lived in the suburbs. To save money the local government was considering turning off sections of streetlights. Things may have been on the decline, but we had a dream that our input could put a new spin on things. Our idea was that if more people saw the real Detroit, the living part, they would feel encouraged to visit and support it. What we needed was a transition from a world where the rule is "It's us or them," to a world where "us" and "them" are no longer separated by a conjunction. To take it one step further, a world where there is no them. Just us.

We arrived at a nearby restaurant and spent the afternoon there half asleep, as if nursing a hangover, eating macaroni and cheese because we were on such a tight budget. *Maybe I shouldn't have given the kids my money*, I lamented to myself.

"So, how do you like my city?" Ben quipped.

"It needs a little work, but that's why we're here, right?" I blurted out.

Levi gave me a nudge. This was his deal and he wanted to do the talking.

"Daniel is tired. Of course we love it and want to document it as best we can."

I jammed macaroni into my mouth and tried to play the silent partner. The room smelled of burnt wood. I gazed at the raised iron railroad signs on the wall.

Levi continued, "Ben, I think if we do this right, we could benefit the city and make a little on the side."

"That's the plan. If we can make a book about how the city is rebuilding itself, I think it would really help," he replied.

We made our way across town to Ben's fourth story flat overlooking the Detroit river. His apartment was simple. There was no television and he cooked most of his meals from scratch in a cast iron skillet. A Pulitzer award sat on the dining room table, a beacon of hope in a fragmented city; a standard, a promise that this man could do something. Levi and I threw down our bags and passed out on the floor. It had been a long drive and we needed to rest. There was an air of respect and I slept well, imagining the sound of the waves in a sea of untapped potential.

The next day we ate breakfast and spoke briefly about the events of the day. The plan was to take a tour of downtown. As we drove through the streets, Ben pointed out old buildings and what used to be inside. We saw both sides of the city, from bustling cafes, bars and restaurants to residential neighborhoods in complete disrepair. Hollywood was in town and had spent the better part of the past few days demolishing old buildings for their next blockbuster. Entire storefronts were blown out and building complexes reduced to rubble in the name of entertainment. It made me sad and angry seeing money being spent to destroy a once great city when it could be being used to rebuild it. I felt that I had once been great too, and now my struggle to become a better man mirrored what we were doing here. Perhaps this book on Detroit would mean redemption on both fronts.

Afterward Levi and I spent some time alone exploring the river near the border with Windsor, Ontario. I walked down an old dock and stared deeply into a grey sky sunk low above the turbulent water. The wind picked up and a flock of geese flew by while a few drops of rain danced across my cheeks. I felt alone standing there at the end of the dock yet filled with peace.

This city was at a turning point. It had to be. All it really needed was someone to encourage it to turn around, to go the other way. I paused and looked down at my knuckles gripping the railing.

This wasn't our job. We were doing the best we could, but to think we could be the difference was ridiculous. I looked back at Levi, preoccupied with photographing an old milk crate stuck in a tree. Who was I trying to fool? We were just two guys living our lives, trying to make a few bucks along the way. This supposed citywide transformation was only going to take three people and a Pulitzer? Unbelievable. As the sun set over the city the glow of the streetlamps made it glitter with life. I pictured the city's power cut and the solitary light from Ben's apartment shining in the night.

On our final morning in Detroit we went to visit some artists converting an old dilapidated house into a space for art exhibits. We climbed to the top of an adjacent building and watched them gut the interior from above. Walking across the roof, I turned and faced Michigan Central Station, a giant structure at the end of a large courtyard which seemed to have nearly every window busted out. Below, hundreds of people were setting up for a giant bean bag toss tournament and a band played loudly on a stage in the distance.

After climbing down, we mingled in the crowd, took photos and ate good food until it was time for us to go. It was great to see that people could still enjoy themselves, their spirit untamed. We said goodbye to Ben and took one last look at the jagged skyline, bidding a fond farewell to Detroit.

I felt hopeful about the future, though a hollowness lingered as I knew I would be returning home to an empty apartment. *Mei might be impressed by our attempts at rebuilding Detroit,* I thought. *Maybe she would finally see potential in me and jump on the next plane to Minneapolis.* It seemed impossible at best and that was discouraging. There was an eerie silence between Levi and I as we made our way back to the Twin Cities. Thoughts of Mei drifted haphazardly through my mind unexpressed.

4

The dry desert wind blows sand in my face as I stand over a large patch of disturbed earth. Men are digging, their sharp metal spades breaking through the fresh dirt. Sweat trickles slowly down the back of my neck and I wipe it with a dirty handkerchief. There is a scent in the air, something musky and foul that reminds me of the blood meal I once used on perennial beds when I worked landscaping as a teenager.

A shovel pierces the loose ground. There is a dull sound as it meets something solid. The man holding it kneels and scrabbles in the earth, throwing clods of it up to the surface. Then, like the unveiling of a painting, he brushes dirt away with his hands. What we are looking at is a human torso. Stumps of a neck, arms, legs. The skin has the look of clay, grey and drained of color. Blood has mixed with the fresh dirt creating muddy blotches on the exposed flesh. The man reaches into the ground and produces a severed head, hair matted with dried blood. One of the ears is missing. Levi's ashen face glares back at me, mouth hanging open and eyes rolled back.

I put the hankie to my mouth, trying to hold back the surge of bile. I turn away, double over, and vomit.

My body convulsed as it was rudely awakened by the dream. I leaned over the side of the bed and gagged. A small amount of stomach acid brimmed up in the back of my throat and made my mouth taste sour.

"What the hell is going on with you?" I said aloud to myself behind clenched teeth.

The image of Levi's dismemberment and the expression on his face caused me to gag again. I shivered. I punched the pillow several times and then rolled over onto my back, pulling the blankets up over my head. My cat jumped onto the edge of the bed, stretched and then curled up in a ball near my feet. I closed my eyes. All I could see was the gore from the dream behind my eyelids. I felt nauseous. I couldn't let these nightmares affect me. I had to go to work in the morning.

Eventually I drifted off into a fitful sleep.

It was 8:02 a.m. when I walked into the office the following morning. One of the maintenance workers stopped me in the hallway.

"Did you get dressed in the dark?"

I issued him a blank stare. "What?"

"You're wearing the wrong hat!"

I removed my cap and turned it in my hands, gently running my fingers over the embroidered yellow M on the crown. I paused for a moment. I had forgotten I was in Minnesota again and the old rivalries still stood.

"I am actually wearing this in support of Detroit. My friend and I are trying to write a book about its recovery."

"You know the University of Michigan isn't in Detroit, right?" He quickly responded.

I wore this hat quite often and you would be surprised how many people badgered me like this. When asked I usually explained that I was not interested in sports and that the hat itself was a symbol to create awareness. That in times of emergency, it is not only necessary but appropriate to cross gaps created by sports rivalries.

"Yeah, I know," I muttered.

I was the lowest ranking member of the asset management department. The previous year I had worked my way up to a permanent position by leading a group of interns through a project that lasted several months. I had inherited a responsibility along with the new position, a challenge to get a massive reorganization project back on track. Giving this task to the newest member confused me at first, though I was just as capable as anyone. They obviously saw great things in me.

The interns themselves were an interesting bunch and included a streetwise hipster, a guy who looked like a lumberjack, several beauty queens and a former basketball player from Kentucky who was second all-time in free throws. I missed our office adventures, though they did come to my isolated cubicle to see me for favors every now and then. I was often told not to, but I always helped them out.

My favorite coworker was a man named Jacob who worked deep in the heart of the office. His weathered, lined face made me think he might possess ancient wisdom. Having survived cancer, he had an enviable inner strength.

He was the man who three decades prior created one of the most beloved images in Minnesota sports history, the newest incarnation of Goldy the Gopher. He had only received a small bonus for his contribution. I don't think he ever realized that his work was displayed in every corner of the city. He acted as though he had never seen it. Around five o'clock you could usually find me hanging around his cubicle, talking, laughing and feeling relieved that the day was almost over. This was one of those days.

"How was your weekend?" Jacob began.

"Great. I ran a half marathon by myself on Saturday."

"Really? That is quite an accomplishment. You know, I was into running back in college. I was pretty good at it. I still go to this park in Saint Paul sometimes. Really nice trails."

"Oh yeah? We should run together sometime!" I replied, trying not to sound excited.

"I don't know, you are so much younger than me. I don't run very fast."

"Oh, come on, I'm not that fast either. I was running ten-minute miles last weekend," I conceded.

"Alright. I'll think about it." he said, laughing at my eagerness. Jacob paused to shuffle through a manila folder on his desk.

"What did you do last week—?" My boss suddenly called from across the office, stopping me mid-sentence as he gestured for me to follow him. "Hold that thought. I'll be back."

I smiled, ducked out of Jacob's cubicle and headed toward the other side of the building.

Jon was a slight man with a full beard and spectacles that seemed to glisten when you looked at him. He was a wizard with code and believed that the system he had created to manage art assets was flawless. I often found myself consumed by his intellect, like an organic cog in a machine of steel. I admired him for his accomplishments and believed he was a very talented man. However, I thought digging ditches was more liberating than the time I was spending hunched over in my cubicle. My position was not even necessary in order to create a product.

Jon was a gifted musician. He wrote songs from time to time for a Christian website that sold gospel music. I had heard a few of them and was impressed that he found time to fit it into his schedule. It seemed so much more human than what he was doing at Lacroix. Sometimes I wondered why he didn't just quit and play the piano in a low-key bar somewhere.

"Do you have the updated metrics?" he asked.

I glanced at the charcoal portrait he had hanging in his office. John F. Kennedy glared ominously back at me; his hands folded at his mouth. I looked down at the crucifix on Jon's desk. I felt awkward and nervous. All I could think of was the late President's assassination. Flashes of death from my dreams ran repeatedly through my head. I began to feel lightheaded.

"Yes, all assets have been processed to 80% completion," I replied, almost robotically.

With my back straight, I tried to make direct eye contact. I could smell death in his office, rotten and stale, stagnant air. Was it a hallucination?

"So, you have made some good progress then?"

"Yes. I also got some of the coding to work on our new spreadsheet." I tried to smile.

"That's great. Is it saved in its usual place?"

"Yes, pull it up and have a look."

I shook my head slightly trying to dispel the images and smells from my mind. Jon picked up on the reaction that seemed to be caused by some kind of muscle memory.

"Is it not in its usual place?" he asked, confused.

"No, it's there. Sorry I just had a knot in my neck," I lied.

We talked for fifteen minutes about ways to streamline his process, but at the end of the day I felt no more passionate about it than I did about office supplies. Two years ago, I had seen myself designing at an ad agency downtown. How had I ended up managing art assets?

I went back to work and cataloged a few more assets, scanning the artwork and running macros before leaving for the day. I powered down my computer and let out a small inaudible sigh. It wasn't a glamorous thing spending the entire day at a desk, and I felt like a weight had been lifted once the screen went black. Now free to wander, my thoughts turned to Mei in her far away office. If I was quick, I could catch her in between her job and graduate school. "Perhaps she is waiting for me to call," I mused. I grabbed my keys and headed for the car.

5

Mei. Her name was the most beautiful I had ever heard. I mouthed it over and again like an incantation. She had been living in Baltimore for several years now. She had an undergrad degree from one of the best universities in the United States and was working on a masters from a prestigious graduate school. She was a consultant for a credit card company. It was a competitive and cruel environment and I wished she would screw it all or just knit those cold people some sweaters. She spent hours at her desk, and even when she got home, she worked at her computer late into the night. It made me sad to think of her that way because I remembered the girl in the high school hallway with the stack of books and the award-winning smile. Did that girl still exist, or had she vanished entirely? She had only begun talking to me recently despite her credentials and higher status in life, a sign that the part of her I cared to discover was still there. I knew that she wasn't happy by the way she responded when we talked on the phone; there was no passion in her voice, no lust for life. It made me paranoid that she wasn't happy talking to me, rather than in general. On the other hand, if she could confide her unhappiness in me, surely that was a sign of closeness? Who was she, really, and why did I feel this way about her? I wanted to know.

I had found Mei again on a social networking site. The thing is, I couldn't remember having a single conversation with her during our time in school. I had always been too awe-struck to initiate anything so intimate. These days we chatted online and by phone, sometimes about inane things like what kind of breakfast cereal we ate. I told her I liked mine mushy and subtle, intending to hint at romance and I hoped she would pick up on this.

The Mei I remembered was young and innocent, but this one seemed strained and reserved. Being Chinese American in the United States was difficult at times because of racist attitudes and stereotypes. Had these influences hardened her and if so, how could I be of comfort? I felt as though she was the answer to a problem that needed solving and I was too shy to ask the question. Listening to the muffled ringing on the end of the line I knew my chances were running out. I coughed several times to clear my throat, unsure of my voice.

"Hi, Mei," I practiced, following it up with a cough.

"Ahem! Hi, Mei."

Still ringing. The butterflies in my stomach were unbearable. Not realizing the phone had picked up, I cleared my throat again.

"Hello?" came the voice on the other line.

"Hi, Mei. It's Daniel!" I finally blurted out.

"Hi, Daniel. I wasn't expecting your call. Is someone else there with you?"

"Haha," I laughed uneasily. "No. Why would there be?"

"I just thought I heard you talking to someone."

"Oh, you know, I was just practicing what I wanted to say."

I was being a little too honest for my own good.

"Practicing? Why?"

"Oh, I don't know. I think I was just losing my voice," I blushed.

Mei giggled.

"I see. Well, you sound alright now."

"Yeah I am fine."

"You are still kind of a goofball, aren't you? I always remembered that about you."

I imagined Mei wrapping a loose strand of hair around her index finger and I thought she might be flirting with me. What if she thought I was too silly for her? I was reminded of an image of her butt in a tight pair of jeans that I had seen on her social media page. I was so ready for her.

"I hope not too much of a goofball. I don't want to be too goofy you know?"

Mei laughed again.

"Why do you think we never talked in school?" I asked.

"I don't know. We were just in different circles I guess," she replied.

"Yeah, you were smart. I wasn't," I admitted.

"I don't know about that. I think it was more like you had fun and I didn't."

"Maybe you're right, but what about now?"

"No, still no fun. I am expected to go out for drinks after work every night though."

In that moment I imagined Mei and I going out on the town, perhaps dressing up and going to a romantic dinner together. Maybe it was the night that I would propose to her. Maybe it was Valentine's Day and afterward we would go back to our shared apartment for an intimate night alone together. My heart was growing fuller by the minute.

"And you don't want to?"

"No, not really," she confessed reluctantly.

"Yeah, me neither."

I didn't tell her the thing I wanted to say, that I thought she was beautiful, that I was in love with her and although this truth hovered over all our interactions, it was unspeakable.

From a young age she had been driven to pursue status and importance instead of her own happiness. I'd known Mei for thirteen years and she had always been a grafter. I thought anyone who spent that much time shuffling through papers and pounding computer keys deserved a little freedom.

"I'm having a little bit of a problem tonight, Daniel."

"What's wrong?" I replied, concerned.

"I am failing one of my classes. I just can't get an F. I've never had one in my entire life."

I found it hard to imagine her receiving a B. It seemed the image I had of Mei in my mind had suddenly cracked and broken. I scrambled to put it back together.

"Believe it or not I have never had an F either. What are you going to do about it?" I asked, trying not to sound too shocked.

"I have no idea. I don't think there is anything I can do."

"Listen, I know you've worked hard to get where you are. I'm sure you could speak to your instructor and do extra work or something like that. You're a genius, I know you can do it."

"Don't flatter me," she said brushing off my compliment. "I am far from that."

"You're closer than I am, trust me."

Mei laughed anxiously.

"It's not a big deal. Really, it's not," I reassured her.

"It's a bigger deal than you think," she trailed off.

I felt awkward. Had my efforts at being supportive betrayed my obsession? Someone so flawless should not be punished for making an error. Although if she was flawless could she even make an error in the first place? During the past few years I had come to understand that there were two kinds of perfection. The first was the natural cycle in which we live, where things rise and fall like the changing of the tides; a perfection which nevertheless contained death, putrefaction and filth. The second, an imaginary place that was created perfect and sentenced to remain so in an impermanent world, as clear and brittle as glass, for the ideal was a place, a locus, even when its template applied to living beings. It seemed as though Mei was held to a high standard her entire life and now, tasked with maintaining perfection well into adulthood, she was faltering. Why had I been offered this insight into her life? Was there anything that I could do to help her? It was only a matter of time before her artificial world would shatter.

I thought for a moment that this change in my perception of her had become an error in her logic rather than my own. Trying to stay as close as I could without disrupting her delicate balance, I was like a distant satellite on a course through the darkness. I was now orbiting her, sending my love as energetic transmissions. Did she receive these even subconsciously? For some reason I felt unwelcome in her life. To lose this central force she wrought would create a void that my nightmares would have no problem filling.

6

Some days after work I volunteered at Folwell, an inner-city middle school in South Minneapolis. I'd been a student worker there for a few years. The district was running short on funding for music, sports and art classes, and I was an assistant coach for the soccer team as well as a teacher for the photography club. Mentors were in short supply here, and the kids needed more protection and guidance. I grew up thinking that bigger cities like Minneapolis and Detroit were full of drug dealers and muggers, but there was more to the city. There were a lot of good people here.

I sat at a desk in the school's front office working on a graphic and chatting with the secretary. A tall Mexican named Carlos sat at the desk next to me filing papers. He was large and intimidating with broad shoulders and neatly trimmed facial hair. He often made references to narcotics which seemed strange in this setting.

"I remember being young at my middle school in Saint Paul," Carlos began. "All the chelitos were afraid of me."

He sounded proud.

"You mean the other children Carlos? Why would they be afraid of you?" the secretary asked.

"Maybe it was because I was bigger than they were or maybe it was because I was slinging juana to all of the high school kids."

"Juana, huh?" she replied, a skeptical look on her face.

I fidgeted in my chair a little and tried to act busy. It was as though a cold draft was crawling through the office. My eyes rolled back in my head. I felt as though I was being tortured by a complex combination of fear and disgust.

"...and what exactly is that?" she prodded.

Of course, she knew what it was.

"Oh, juana is slang for tarjetas de béisbol. Baseball cards," he replied with a guttural chuckle.

"Whatever..." I muttered under my breath, suddenly snapping out of it.

When he reminisced about drugs the secretary and I gave each other funny looks. It wasn't really my responsibility to challenge him but on the other hand, if I didn't remain protective and vigilant, the kids might end up in the same kind of trouble I did.

Suddenly the office door swung open and the Spanish liaison, Raquel, walked into the room. Everyone stopped what they were doing and stared up at her. She glided effortlessly past the large metal administrative desks. She was a fiery Colombian with a passion for her Latino community. Having fought the prejudice that came with the immigration crisis she was doubly watchful of the kids. I thought she was amazing, though I once correctly predicted a win over Colombia in the World Cup and thought she was going to kill me.

She looked serene as she greeted everyone and the bubbles in her pale blue eyes sparkled. Carlos turned to her and muttered something in Spanish. Her expression immediately became serious as if hearing some pressing news. I didn't know what they were talking about, but I figured it must have been important. She strode behind me and looked over my shoulder.

"What are you working on?" she asked.

I pulled up a window and showed her a poster I had been designing for the school.

"Cool! I have a project I would like help with. Do you have time to have coffee with me this weekend?" she asked, smiling.

I turned around quickly and for a brief moment I thought she was giving me a look.

"Yes!" I said, with a little too much enthusiasm.

I suddenly felt very excited. My head grew light and my stomach churned. Was Raquel interested in me?

"Daniel, you don't go out much, do you?"

"No. I mean, sometimes. I guess I am not as young as I used to be."

I felt a bead of sweat dribble down one of my armpits. "Oh god," I thought. Do I smell?

"Do you ever have fun?"

This sounded familiar. I immediately thought of Mei.

"Of course, I do. I just think my idea of fun may be a little different."

"You are different, aren't you?" she snickered, giving me another sly look.

I scribbled her number on a piece of paper and carefully tucked it into my shirt pocket. I wasn't accustomed to getting requests like this, but I was happy to help. She often asked me to walk down the hall and talk about the future of the noisy children passing us. I kind of liked her, though my feelings for Mei prevented me from making any advances.

We met on a Saturday morning. We were both heavily in debt with school loans and she had an idea to start a business in order to pay hers off. In Latin America they had a special service called Animadores, a group of DJs, musicians and performers that threw parties for people. I thought it was a great idea.

I had done some research the night before and formed a plan for a business identity.

"So, have you had a lot of interactions with these groups?" I asked.

"Yes, they are quite popular in Latin America," Raquel replied.

"…I noticed there weren't many businesses like that in the US when I was doing my research."

"I think we will be the only ones in the Twin Cities."

"Oh, WE will, will we?" I laughed.

"Yeah. You're in, right?"

I blushed. Why was Raquel doing this now? This beautiful Columbian was sitting right in front of me, asking me if I was with her and all I could think about was Mei. An image of Raquel taking me into a stall in the women's bathroom and having her way with me passed through my mind. What the hell? What was I thinking? I lowered my head, looked at my feet under the table and paused for a moment before I answered her.

"Don't hesitate. Don't think about it. Just say yes!" she laughed.

"Yeah, okay okay," I brushed her off a little.

Her face grew sour.

"Don't sound so excited. Jeez, Daniel."

Did she mean this romantically? I couldn't tell for sure. My mind seemed to betray my thoughts of Mei as images of Raquel sitting poolside in a bikini swirled around in my head.

"What exactly are you going to have me do?" I questioned.

"Hah. Wouldn't you like to know?" she laughed.

"Yeah, actually I would."

"Top secret," she giggled.

"I can't sign up for something I don't know about," I frowned a little.

"All in good time, Daniel. All in good time."

She placed her fingertips together and made a triangular shape with her hands.

We sipped coffee for another hour or so and after a while we discussed going out to a local bar for an afternoon drink. I followed her in my car to the pub and we walked in together. The waitress brought a

Bloody Mary for Raquel and a cola for me. I tried to play it cool, doing my best to navigate the conversation.

"What's the worst hangover you've ever had?" I asked Raquel.

"Well, I don't know about hangovers. I have had a lot. Once I had something, we call Montezuma's revenge from drinking bad water in Colombia. I was in bed for days and throwing up every half hour. It was awful."

Her story made her seem less attractive. I chuckled a little.

"What about you?" Raquel asked, leaning over the table. I could smell a hint of sandalwood on her skin. I immediately forgot about Montezuma's revenge, imagining the smell being caught in my bed sheets and remaining there for days afterwards.

"Well, I overdosed on drugs once."

"Daniel! What the heck? I thought you were a good boy!" Raquel exclaimed.

"Oh, you would be surprised. I have all sorts of skeletons."

She seemed to be more amused than surprised. It must have felt good to have a little dirt on a guy who appeared squeaky clean

"Do you want to go to a party? Carlos from work will be there," Raquel offered.

Carlos? I had other ideas.

"Well I was planning on going running with a friend. I don't really want to be out all night," I explained.

I was crazy for turning her down, but it was true. Carlos was a deal breaker. What kind of party was this?

"Oh, come on, I want to hang out with you more."

I sighed, not wanting her to push it. Mei once again dominated my inner dialogue. *Mei, Mei, Mei, Mei*, I mentally repeated to myself.

"Okay. I am never going to get you to come out of your shell. I accept it," she retreated, crossing her arms.

When our drinks were finished, we paid our tabs and walked slowly into the parking lot. I felt as though she didn't want to let me go so soon. We stopped just short of her car, lingering under the shade of an oak tree that was hanging out over the near empty sea of asphalt.

"I have something for you. Just a minute."

She opened the trunk and pulled out a poster advertising the Day of the Dead celebration in one of the nearby Latino neighborhoods. She smiled.

"I know it's kind of far off, but I thought you might like to put it somewhere."

"Thanks. It would look nice on a wall in my apartment."

"Alright, good. You will be that much more cultured," she smirked.

Despite having a good time with Raquel, I was looking for someone different, someone smarter or more grown up. Someone like Mei. Raquel was just a girl who hung out with kids all day, not that I thought it was a bad thing. I just wanted something more. Even if I was sexually attracted to her, I felt I could keep my impulses under wraps. But the next day I found out that she didn't go to the party either. Maybe, just maybe I was rubbing off on her. I didn't want to admit it, but it made me like her more. "A future with Raquel," I was beginning to think. "There was an idea."

7

I pulled my running shoes out of the car and sat down to tie them. Though he was over 60 years old, I had convinced Jacob to go running with me. I found myself running several miles almost every day and it had become a form of therapy. It was a small consolation that eclipsed Mei's void, if only temporarily. Jacob pulled up in his tan sport utility vehicle. Despite his age he was still fit and strong.

"How is it going today, my friend?" Jacob asked.

He sat down on a nearby bench to tie his shoes. I grabbed my ankle and stretched my leg.

"The sky is blue and it's sunny. What more do we need?"

We started out at a steady pace, so we could talk. He asked probing questions. I told him a lot about my family, a suppurating wound of a subject.

"So, tell me about your brother, the one who's been bothering you."

I had trouble talking about it; thoughts of him tore and scraped like rusty metal. I'd been a clever child. I was happy enough back then, spending my days with other bright kids. I was enrolled in gifted and talented classes and was generally well accepted. My brother Russ, however, was a dominant force in my life. My parents divorced when I was two years old, making Russ the alpha male in my mother's household. His moodiness was a gloomy cloud hanging over our home. His sudden bursts of anger made it feel like a war zone. The aggression would sometimes turn to blows, and on more than one occasion my head would meet the sharp edges of shelves and tables as I ricocheted around the room.

"I can't believe you dwell on this stuff so much. You're young, you're a great guy and you have some good years ahead of you. You should be out with people your age, not running trails with an old guy like me," Jacob continued.

He had more of a point than he knew, though I preferred his company.

"Don't take this the wrong way but I want you to adopt me," I laughed.

I was scholastic and artistic in school, qualities that Russ never valued. When I was in second grade, I had a solo in a choral arrangement. I sang that I would be a defender of my planet and that united with friends I would save the Earth. I believed the words I sang. But it was kind of a joke to Russ because singing didn't really solve anything. Men were supposed to be silent and masculine. I was more of the friendly type who liked to smile a lot. Russ decided that I must be gay.

I didn't get it at age ten. According to him I needed to be tough. He taught me this lesson with violence. He would pick me up over his head and throw me on the ground, tossing me around the room like a rag doll. He devised a game in which he would block me into a corner of the house and force me to find my way past him. When I would refuse to play, he would sit on my chest, force me to open my mouth and try to spit into it. Sometimes he would hit me and slam me back into the corner. Sometimes he would shove my face into the floor until I got carpet burns on my cheeks. My screaming summoned the police one time; the neighbors could no longer tolerate it. But despite this, I didn't listen to Russ's bad advice. My mom never intervened because she was afraid of Russ's size and strength. She would try to ground him for his violence, but he would never follow her orders. There wasn't much she could do. I would often withdraw into my bedroom, playing with Lego blocks for hours by myself. It was the safest place left in the house even though the door was practically busted off the hinges from times when Russ tried to forcibly enter. Sometimes it prompted me to hide in the closet, but after a while the folding closet door sat propped up against the wall, off the hinges and broken from Russ trying to fling it open one too many times. My sanctuary was an unsafe place.

Perhaps if I hadn't been bullied this way, I would never have taken drugs. I would be with Mei right now. After a while the scars on my heart became a map to guide me along with patience and common sense. I needed to know the truth about why these things happened. I needed to find out how to stop them.

"So, is he giving you trouble? Do you still talk to him?" Jacob asked.

"No, not really. It just bothers me from time to time."

It bothered me more than he knew. My body tensed up as I was running. I could feel my teeth and fists clenching. My head felt as though a railroad spike had been driven through it.

"And how do your siblings feel about him?"

"Well, my sister Jordan doesn't have much of a problem with him. She doesn't like what he did to me but what can she do? She still loves her brother."

"You just have the two siblings?" Jacob asked, curious.

"Yeah. Just Russ and Jordan."

"So, this was mostly just a problem for you and your mom," Jacob breathed heavily, jumping nimbly over a stray branch. "There comes a point when you just have to say out of sight, out of mind."

"I know. It's just that…" I trailed off.

We ran on through the thick summer foliage. The leaves blurred into a burgeoning mass as I sorted through my muddled thoughts. I knew that when I arrived home I would need to rest in bed for a while.

Thoughts of Russ seemed to be very debilitating and tended to manifest in different ways physically.

"It's hard to know what to say to someone who you believe ruined your life."

"I imagine it is," he replied.

I glanced at him. His gaze was focused straight ahead, inviting my confidence.

I knew I couldn't blame Russ for everything. I felt that everyone had a choice. He had recently married, with a stepson he showered with love and a homosexual brother-in-law. It was clear that he had learned his lesson, but the old scars were still there, and the relationship remained broken. There was nothing wrong with me and it was unfortunate that it had taken me this long to figure that out. The buzzing of the cicadas through the branches of the forest was near deafening. Despite this, there was an awkward silence as we continued running.

Jacob suddenly cleared his throat to speak. The pain seemed to vanish as soon as the thought of him changing the subject arose.

"All of these hills sort of remind me of running up and down the old stadium steps at the University of Minnesota."

"What were your college years like?" I asked, interested.

"Well, I was really athletic. I loved working out at the stadium and lifting weights. I also chased a lot of girls before I met my wife, though I think that is pretty common. By the way, what is going on with you? Why don't you have a girlfriend?"

"Well there is a girl at Folwell I am helping with design work. I don't know if I am going to become her employee or start a combination Partridge Family slash Harlem Globetrotters style soccer team. There is also a girl I kind of like in Baltimore but she's too far away."

He paused for a moment, deep in thought.

"I don't know these women. My advice would be to just go after one," he advised. "I know it can be tough, but I think you should try to settle down."

"That's something I probably need to hear," I breathed out. "Do you want to go get a burger or something after this?"

"Ah, well…" Jacob trailed off a little. "I don't have a ton of time today and I am kind of doing the vegetarian thing. I had cancer, remember?"

"Oh!" I exclaimed. "Maybe I will cook something for you sometime then. I am doing this thing where I cook a different soup every week."

"That would be appreciated but not necessary," he gave me a wink.

We had reached the parking lot. We stretched near the cars while people played tennis nearby.

"Good run," Jacob said, breathing slightly harder than usual.

"Yeah. You're not bad for an old man," I joked.

I imagined myself in Jacob's position. Would I be working at Lacroix until I was his age? I admired Jacob's wisdom, but I wasn't sure I liked the idea of being stuck in that office all my life. *If I could be like Jacob…* I pondered. *Maybe I could handle it. By the time I was his age maybe I would be free from shame and Russ would be having these painful thoughts about me.* I bent over placing my hands on my knees.

"Do it again sometime?" I asked, staring up at Jacob.

"Sure," he smiled warmly, and after saying goodbye, we both drove away into the hot afternoon.

8

On Tuesday mornings the asset management team gathered for a weekly meeting. I hadn't been to many and was eager to be more involved in the company. We sat at the massive table as Jon's boss enquired about our current timetables.

"So, how long do you think it will be before this project is complete?" his boss asked, glaring across the table at me.

Jon's boss was new, like me, and oversaw restructuring the company to make it more profitable. He reminded me of a schoolyard bully. I kept this thought on lockdown, as though his gaze could penetrate my skull. I definitely didn't want to cross him.

"According to my data we should be done sometime in December," I informed him.

"I thought we were projecting September after our initial planning in the Spring."

"I know but I was pulled off to keyword large batches of assets." I continued. "I also had to spend a few days watching tutorials for the new cataloging system, as well as building spreadsheets to organize the new data."

It hardly amounted to being three months late. My confidence was fading. I shifted uneasily in my chair and cautiously let my vision wander over the other faces at the table. I felt apathetic eyes staring back at me, apathetic about whether I was here or not, knowing that if I were gone, I could be easily replaced tomorrow.

"Why didn't we have extra time built into our projections?" he asked.

"This was my first project. I wasn't sure what to expect as far as additional work."

"Yeah, I can see that," he frowned, scribbling something down in his notebook.

Nervously, I blurted out the most random thing I could think of to change the subject.

"Have we ever used the keywords 'bathtub' or 'pineapple' for any of our assets? I noticed them in the catalog."

My coworkers stared at me blankly.

"Jon, do you have any more information about the new software?"

He had changed the subject. The conversation moved on.

I couldn't help it if I seemed out of place. The meeting was long and boring and made me feel as though I was being waterboarded. We sat for two hours at the long table with the canvas covered office chairs. I often found myself daydreaming about Mei as I tried not to stick the end of my pen in my mouth. Was she sitting in a similar meeting? Probably, I thought, clicking the pen a few times.

I imagined she was the one at the front of the room giving the presentation. She looked sexy in her business clothes as she undid her hair and the top few buttons of her blouse.

"You know I always liked naughty boys," she cooed seductively as she crawled onto the table.

She slowly slinked her way past my horrified coworkers on her hands and knees until she reached me. She ran her hand across my cheek and touched my lips. She curled up into my lap and began kissing my neck and nibbling my ear.

She whispered, "Won't you be my bad boy now, Danny?"

Mei shoved her hand down my pants.

I squirmed a little to keep myself from getting excited. *Snap out of it, Daniel!* I looked down and made sure my shirt was adequately covering my crotch. *Get serious*, I thought. *You are so behind!*

I had to be determined to stay positive about our project. I would simply work faster and stay later. In the grand scheme of things organizing assets wasn't a big deal. There was nothing to worry about.

As everyone filed out of the conference room Jon pulled me aside. I tried to smile because he didn't look angry.

"Don't worry, Daniel. You'll catch up," he reassured me.

"Yeah. I know I will, too. It will just take time."

His face grew severe for a brief moment.

"No more jokes, okay?"

"Okay, okay," I replied, my voice trailing off.

He smiled and put his hand on my shoulder, striding by at his usual pace. He was always running around the office "putting out fires," as he called it. It was all I could do to keep from fanning the flames. I followed him with ironic slowness. I noticed Jacob working quietly in his cubicle. I poked my head around the cubicle wall.

"Hey, Jacob. Do you have a minute?"

"Sure, Daniel. What's up?" he asked as he squinted at the screen, manipulating artwork.

"Well, it was supposed to be a surprise."

He looked up from his work.

"This isn't about you trying to get Hormel to build a Superbowl ring out of Spam, is it? If you keep trying to pull things like that you're going to get fired."

I couldn't help it that the Minnesota Vikings had never won a Superbowl. For a while I became so sick of hearing everyone complain about them I decided to try to get them the ring myself. No one ever said it had to be made of metal. I tried to look innocent.

"Uh, no. It's not about that."

"Well, what is it?" he said, sounding a little annoyed. "I'm kind of busy right now."

"Do you remember what you said to me about the stadium steps?" I asked.

"Yeah. How could I forget?"

He tilted his head a little so he could see beyond his glasses.

"I emailed the University and told them who you are. I asked them if we could run on the steps of the new stadium sometime."

"You did? What did they say?" he inquired, now giving me his full attention.

"They said we could tour the stadium but running on the steps would be a problem."

"That's too bad. Thanks for the thought."

He didn't seem disappointed.

"I was really hoping they would let us," I said feeling a little defeated.

"Listen. Let's just keep that between you and me, and you have to promise me something."

"What's that?"

"I want you to keep your job here. Promise me you will just do it and quit all the theatrics. I know you are bored but you're going to get in big trouble if you keep emailing people as though you were a Lacroix HR representative. We'll talk later, alright?"

Two warnings in a row? I was about to strike out. Feeling ashamed of myself I looked down to see a crucifix on Jacob's desk, almost exactly the same cross as the one I had seen on Jon's.

"Alright. Thanks for running with me," I replied, feeling repulsed.

It was clear I needed help from these men. I distinctly got the feeling that they would only help me if I were Christian. It was true that I had been raised Catholic, but what if I wanted to be something else? Were they forcing me into a mold, shaping me into their ideal employee or coworker? Even though it was my job I didn't feel so good about where

I was being led. I imagined that I was in the Spanish inquisition and these two men were interrogating me, trying to discover if my soul was worth saving. The image in my mind caused me to feel a panicked sense of dread.

"Not a problem," Jacob replied.

I turned the corner around the cubicle and paused for a moment. Trying to calm myself I bowed my head and put my hand on my chest. With the opposite hand on the wall of the cubicle I let out a heavy sigh. I knew he was serious. Maybe Jon had talked to him about my progress. Jacob had told me once that they were close friends, and after seeing their twin crosses I had no doubt. It was confusing because they seemed so different. The fun was over. I needed to get real. This job was keeping me alive.

"You alright buddy?" one of the artists asked in passing.

"Yeah, I just need a breather," I replied, pulling myself together.

"Keep at it!" he returned, ducking into a nearby cubicle.

I walked back to my desk and fell into my chair. I briefly navigated through a thick pile of file folders, knowing this wasn't going to be easy. Nothing good ever was.

Corners Untouched by Madness

Daniel

9

Under the glow of streetlights, a beat-up truck pulls onto a remote bridge. A man emerges and rounds the vehicle, removing two large, musky burlap sacks from the back. He sets them down on the ground. Dark liquid from the damp bags mingles with the puddles in the potholes in the weathered concrete, sending small sanguine strands out into the muddy, disturbed water. He pauses and looks around. For an instant he thinks he hears something. After a moment, he throws the sacks over the railing into the cloudy waters below. He leans over into the darkness surveying the ripples. Then he turns, enters his vehicle and slams the door. A miasma of dust in the glow of the taillights then nothing.

I woke up feeling tortured. My cat clawed my face and I nearly jumped out of bed, my heart pounding in my chest. I anxiously wiped the sweat from my brow. It was cool and must have been gathering there for some time as I slept. My sheets were also moist with perspiration and I squirmed a little to kick them off myself. I lay there alone for a long moment, half-naked and afraid. The nightmares were becoming more frequent and I felt that I was a part of the problem. *Maybe I could use my past experiences with drugs to educate people about addiction and the drug war in Mexico,* I thought. *Maybe that would appease the dreams.*

I turned on the bedside light and left the room to grab paper and a pen. The conclusion I arrived at was that in order to end the nightmares I would have to create something that would counteract my past. To make a short film about immigration reform and the war on drugs in Mexico was my midnight epiphany. The ghosts in the dreams wanted truth and I feared that if I didn't do something soon, the nightmares would never end. Living in fear was not really living after all. I couldn't let my shadow keep me intimidated. Fear seemed absurd.

I did some research the next day and wrote a script for a thirty-minute film. In daydreams I began planning where I would shoot footage. I asked Levi to lend me his video camera because all I had was a digital point and shoot. It had been a while since I last saw him. After arriving home from Detroit, the project was put on the back burner. We needed time to gather funding. The people of Detroit weren't depending on us. This was a difficult thought somehow. Our book probably wouldn't have any impact on the severity of their struggle. It was a letdown at best. Levi answered the door as his children peeked out from behind the curtain of their porch window.

"Hey, stranger. Where have you been?" he asked, his dark eyes squinting in the sunlight.

"Around, I guess. How are you doing?" I replied.

"Good. Still waiting on Detroit. So, you want to borrow my camera? What's this secret project you are planning?"

"It's nothing. I just want to take some footage around the city for a short film."

"Really? What's it about?" he asked.

"Immigration."

He raised an eyebrow as Anna appeared beside him.

I continued, "I just wanted to talk about why immigrants are coming here illegally, you know, running from drug cartels and seeking better lives for their families. I feel like they are dehumanized. I also want to denounce the drug violence in Mexico and Latin America."

"I see," Levi replied.

"A film, huh? Do you have any experience with filmmaking?" Anna quizzed.

"Well no, but I don't think it will cost any money. If we can't get started on Detroit, I'd like to find something to occupy my time," I explained.

"Knock yourself out then," Levi smirked.

He threw the camera over to me. I didn't want to tell him that my feelings about my dreams and my past addictions were a big problem for me. It was causing me to withdraw further into my shell. Why did it bother me so much? I tried to lie to myself about it but it was slowly becoming clear that the dreams really were beginning to scare me. Dealing with this was part of being an adult, right?

"You need a girlfriend, Daniel," Anna piped up. "Why don't you go on a dating website?"

"Well, I don't know. This is just for fun. Since when was a girlfriend everyone's solution to everything?"

"Oh, I just think it might be good for you to meet someone."

"It probably would be," I said gritting my teeth a little. This was getting old.

"Anyone is better than that last girlfriend you had. What was her name? Fiona?"

"Felicia," I corrected her.

"Oh yes, Felicia. Whatever happened to her?"

"I have no idea," I replied, annoyed.

Anna shooed the kids away from the window. I tried to hold my tongue about any details on the film. I could tell they wanted to see me happy, but I felt like the chaos developing in my life would set them up for disappointment.

"So, do you have any prospects?" Anna asked, prodding a little.

I immediately thought of Mei but since we hadn't talked for a while, I felt uncertain about bringing her up. I racked my brain for a few more moments and suddenly remembered Raquel. I had forgotten about her. I pulled out my phone and found a picture I had taken of her for one of my posters.

"This is Raquel. I work with her at Folwell and we have a little project going together."

"Wow, she's cute!" exclaimed Levi.

Anna nudged him.

"I kind of had my eye on someone else though," I said, looking down at the floor.

"Don't worry about that. At least there is someone," she simpered, apparently satisfied.

"Yeah," I replied quietly.

"You know, back in high school I had the hots for both of you guys. Levi was my number one though."

I looked at Levi and he shrugged.

"Well, I for one am glad you got what you wanted. I had other interests."

"Oh really? Like who?"

My face turned red.

"No one you knew," I lied.

"Try me. I knew everyone."

"Never mind," I muttered.

When I got back into the car my mind was swimming. I remembered now that I had promised Raquel I would meet with her about Animadores. I had forgotten all about it until Anna inadvertently caused me to bring her up. Leaving Levi to idle had freed up some time but I hadn't realized how full my plate really was. I drove down Marshall, into Minneapolis, hitting every red light along the way until it turned into Lake Street. I needed time to think. When I pulled into

Folwell's parking lot I sat for a long moment gripping the steering wheel.

"Pull it together, Daniel. You can do this," I urged myself, banging on the wheel a few times. I began to feel ill.

I walked past a dumpster and up a loading dock. Suddenly losing my nerve and becoming dizzy, I doubled over beside the large rusted trash can and gagged. Nothing came out but a few guttural coughs. I squatted down for a moment with one hand on the massive cement slab and the other cradling the computer bag hanging from my shoulder.

"It's just nerves. It will pass," I mouthed

I wasn't immediately sure why I felt this way, but I knew it had something to do with Raquel. Were my feelings for her making me anxious or was it something else? I felt overwhelmed by the thought of her. I remained outside the school for a few minutes. When I finally entered the building, the hallways were empty and my footsteps bounced off the cream-colored walls, filling the deserted school with an even tempo. I found Raquel at her desk checking her email.

"Hey, Raquel!" I exclaimed hesitantly, tapping on the doorframe. "Do you want to see the Animadores logo? It's almost finished."

"Yeah, show me what you've got," she replied, turning to face me.

I took my laptop out of my bag and opened it, pulling up the logo I had created for her new company. She looked and smiled one of the biggest smiles I had ever seen. It wasn't one you saw very often, and it was worth the effort just to see it.

"It looks awesome!" she grinned. "I can't wait to get started. Do you still want to paint the kids' faces?"

"Well, maybe."

"Daniel, you said you would! In fact, I might need you to paint a booth. My sister is really good at art too, so maybe she could help you do stuff like that."

I started getting worried. When was I going to find time for all of this? The soccer season was just beginning, and work wasn't going so well. My film wasn't too important, but it was something I really wanted to do. What about the Detroit project? I was beginning to realize why I had felt so overwhelmed. "Just focus on one thing," I thought.

The logo had a girl in a fedora, a man dancing and another with a boombox under a spotlight. It was colorful and the girl in the fedora made me think of Raquel. I reminded myself that helping her with something like Animadores would possibly have a positive outcome, maybe even more so than a film.

"Well, just finish up and we'll go from there. We can meet after school sometime. I'm almost always here so just come find me."

"Sounds good," I said, putting the computer back into my bag.

I walked out into the silent hallway and climbed a large stone staircase. I turned my borrowed key in the lock of the computer lab. I loved working at Folwell. Maybe if I had stayed, I would be closer to Raquel. Perhaps I would even be her boyfriend.

I sat in a small plastic chair with my feet on one of the desks, bright squares of sunshine on the floor. The printer hummed softly in the background and as I closed my eyes my worries rolled away. Feeling overwhelmed at times was normal, wasn't it? Sure, a lot of things were set against me early on, but I had a good job and some meaning in my life. So, what if things were a little out of control? I leaned back a little so two of the chair legs were no longer touching the ground. Animadores, Detroit, the film, Lacroix. It all had to get done or at least I wanted it done. What was I going to give up? Where would I have to break? It was clear that Lacroix had to stay. I wondered if my footing was firmly planted in the company though.

I was becoming lost in my aspirations, unsure where to go next. I could just say fuck it all and move to southeast Asia, spending the rest of my days on a remote beach just outside Pattaya. It wasn't realistic but I liked the idea. My life in the Twin Cities seemed to be headed in a difficult direction. "It's only temporary. In another year this will all be straightened out. You can get it all done," I tried to comfort myself. I didn't feel comforted though, only a serious sense of doubt about the future and where my life was headed.

10

The next day I drove to Saint Paul and stepped into the cool morning of the Midway streets. I decided I wasn't retreating again. I was going to throw myself headfirst into the fear inspired by my dreams of violence. Midway was not dangerous but over the years it had grown dilapidated and a little rough around the edges. I visited often because Levi and Anna lived nearby.

I walked around the neighborhood, taking footage of the people and places in an effort to depict the culture and pride that these communities had to offer. University Avenue was completely torn up to make way for the new light rail and the place looked like hell. I walked past an alley beside a club where a group of people were painting a mural. I stopped to film a giant sculpture of a heron made from scrap metal. It made me think of all the bad and unwanted parts of life coming together to make something beautiful. This was the narrative I was aiming for, but I felt insecure. This place was their home after all, not mine. I loitered on the sidewalk close to a bus stop, taping the traffic as a man heckled me.

"You see that guy in the picture?" the stranger asked with a thick African accent.

"You mean the ad on the bus stop?" I replied hesitantly.

"Yeah, he is my cousin. You see his face? He says 'leave me alone'."

What the fuck was that? Did this guy have it in for me? I nervously hurried down the street, glancing behind me every now and then. Was this man part of the cartel? Did he know what I was doing? Feeling intimidated and a little frightened, I stopped at the end of the block. I stood for a moment and admired a small school with a front walk covered in colorful chalk outlines. I decided that if this was going to work, I would need to be braver. I gathered the courage to turn around. Upon reaching the stoop I encountered a group of people that had formed in the entryway. Wading through them I approached the unfamiliar African man who had called out to me.

"Hey, I just wanted to apologize for intruding. My name is Daniel. I am making a film about immigration in the Twin Cities."

He pulled a soda can from behind his back and took a sip.

"It's okay. We don't get many people walking around with video cameras. I actually immigrated here from Africa, so I am glad you said something."

"Yeah, I understand. It is hard to get citizenship and even harder to face the immigrant stigma. Being a minority in the United States is still a full-time job," I said, smiling.

He frowned and I could tell he didn't want to discuss this.

"What do you know about being a minority?"

Embarrassed, I quickly responded, "Not enough."

He gave one final laugh as I left him to continue his watch.

I squirmed back through the crowd and out onto the street. After walking up and down University Avenue for two hours I hopped in my car, looking for more subject matter. I decided to head to Cesar Chavez, one of the biggest Latin American communities in the state. Maybe the answer that would unlock the riddle of my nightmares was hidden there.

When I arrived, I parked near a Mexican restaurant with a statue of Charlie Brown outside. He was wearing a sombrero, a poncho and a thick black mustache. There were murals depicting Latin art on nearly all the buildings and the colors were vibrant unlike the rest of the city. It was like stepping into a little piece of Mexico, a country I wanted to see safe from its own violent history. I had never been there and because of the dreams I was not sure how my psyche would handle visiting.

The street was dotted with laborers wearing cowboy hats, leaning against the street signs and telephone poles. I imagined they were waiting for someone to pick them up and give them a job repairing houses or doing yard work. Wasn't that illegal? Maybe they would even kill someone for a price. I swallowed hard. Nervously, I walked past them, approaching a small food cart. The vendor was selling a corn on the cob style dish sprinkled with cheese. His thick black mustache concealed his mouth as he spoke to me in broken English.

"You want? Two dollars."

"Would you mind if I videotaped you?" I said, gesturing toward the camera.

For a moment he wasn't sure what to do. After some careful consideration he went inside a nearby building and emerged with a small boy.

"Do you mind if I videotape you?" I asked.

The man motioned to the boy and nodded. I guessed he was around eleven years old, short for his age, a little pudgy with an uneasy smile.

"Yes, that would be okay," the boy replied.

He seemed shy but was a good intermediary.

"How long have you guys had this stand?" I continued.

"A few years. Are you with the government?" the boy asked timidly.

I had trouble discerning whether it would be a good thing if I were.

"Um, I have campaigned for the president a little but not technically."

I turned the camera off for a moment and then continued.

"So, can I have some corn then?"

"Sure!" the boy said smiling.

I wasn't sure if they understood that I wasn't with any organization, something lost in translation. I still felt like I was an unwanted guest. Most Latino communities were somewhat guarded due to prejudice from mainstream American society. They looked out for each other. A Mexican family had once taken me in to feed and protect me when I was struggling through school. Hardly even knowing who I was, they offered me everything they had like it had always been mine. My gratitude to them was a guiding force behind what I was doing now. I felt that since they looked out for me I would return the favor. Maybe doing something positive for the community at large would help them somehow. Maybe I could garner enough attention to get them to notice me. They would hail me as their savior and make me the leader of the Cinco De Mayo festival

I drove down Robert Street to get some footage outside of the Minnesota State Capitol building. I walked around the courtyard, filming in the cool evening air. The streetlights flicked on one by one, filling the empty streets with a warm glow. The fact that the building was now illuminated didn't make it seem any less deserted.

"At least I am doing something," I thought to myself as I walked back to the car. It honked as the remote opened the locks. As I sat in the driver's seat, I felt a subtle vibration in my pocket. It was Levi.

"Hey Daniel, what are you up to tonight? I thought maybe you could come over for dinner and we could talk about Detroit."

"Can I get a raincheck?" I replied. "I am using your camera to shoot footage as we speak."

"I think it's great that you are so ambitious. Just remember that you're only one person. Don't try to change too much."

Levi was trying to be considerate. I shifted the phone to my shoulder, attempting to turn the engine over. Did he think I was wasting my time? Perhaps he would be jealous if my film produced more fame and respect than anything we could ever do together.

"You don't think one person can change things?" I replied.

"Well, I don't think making an amateur film is going to do much. Can't you just wait for Detroit? Why don't you come have dinner with us? Anna is making her famous guacamole and she wanted to invite you personally. She knows you love that stuff."

"I don't know. This is all I can think to do. I can show you what I have later if you want. Tell Anna to give me a rain check too."

"Alright. Good luck. If you need anything else let us know."

I drove out of the city. When I neared a park overlooking the river I decided to pull over and take some final shots. Lights on bridges and buildings twinkled. There was a feeling of peace, uncommon in such a busy city. I pulled out the camera, trying to capture the spirit of Saint Paul before the light from the sun was completely gone.

At this point I didn't have any tangible plans for my project. Entire armies had difficulties winning the drug war. Was it a mistake to try? *It can't hurt*, I thought. I felt as though my experience in these neighborhoods had given me some perspective on what life was like there. These places that I had once considered to be dangerous or scary when I was growing up in my tiny midwestern hometown did not seem so intimidating to me now. I put the camera away, gazing out across the city. The sound from the freeway was soothing, the rush of rubber against asphalt drowning my fear.

11

Folwell was playing Sanford at soccer and I was one of the only people who knew the rules well enough to referee. It was a clear fall afternoon and the kids were gathering for some friendly competition. They were mostly from Somalia and loved the game more than anything. Helping the young Somalis adapt to American life was important to me. I fantasized that as soccer players they had immediately become tiny diplomats who taught people about their country's strife.

I glanced across the field to see Raquel standing on the sideline. She watched her Latino boys run around with their Somali counterparts, yelling out to them every now and then. It was part of her job to attend these games and it was nice to see her in action. The children ran back and forth. The dust flew up from the large patches of dry dirt dispersed between swaths of grassy field. After the game was over, we lined up at the midfield so that all of the kids could shake hands. Raquel walked up to me slowly, smiling with her hands halfway in her pockets.

"So, I have some news for you."

"Yeah? What's that?" I replied, dropping my referee's whistle down my shirt collar.

"I have a new project for you to help me with. Do you have a minute?"

"Sure, I guess so," I replied, a little uneasily.

I began to feel sick. I knew I didn't have any time for it. What else could I say? There was either something about her or I was just a pushover. I couldn't decide which. It seemed as though she was bad for my health.

We walked the few blocks back to the school from the field. The kids were horsing around and laughing. When I was coaching or refereeing it was like I became a different person. My voice was more commanding, and Raquel had commented on how she had liked seeing this different side of me. It seemed that men and women were playing a game that, unlike soccer, I didn't understand but its intuited rules wouldn't permit me to say no to Raquel.

When we reached the school Raquel and I left the kids. They went to the locker room while we climbed the stone staircase up to the computer lab. I sat down behind a desk and she began scribbling an idea for a new company on a piece of scratch paper.

"Why did you give up on Animadores?" I asked, frowning a little.

The corners of her mouth curled upward slightly.

"I decided that I wanted to work more with kids, so I thought opening up a place to throw parties for them would be better. I have some new ideas about direction. Let me show you."

"I know what it's like switching directions on a project," I continued. "I just feel bad because it was such a good idea."

"I like this idea more. Just do the logo and I will let you know if we need anything else as far as design goes," she replied.

I suddenly got the feeling that Raquel wasn't really interested in me past her business plans. I felt defeated and used. Why did women do this? Why had I gone along with it in the first place? Just to be nice? My stomach turned over and I felt a cold bead of sweat run down my back. I had to say no to her or risk my own sanity.

"Listen, I might not have time for this—" I began.

Determined, she bit her bottom lip as she wrote on a piece of notepaper. It was a floor plan for a space with areas for play equipment, dancing and birthday parties. She finished quickly and handed me the scribbled design.

"Just give me some doodles then. This drawing should give you a better idea."

I was getting worried now. The more I thought about it the more overwhelming my life became. I shoved the slip of paper into my bag.

"I don't know if—"

"Sounds good," she interrupted. "Sorry to cut this short but I have to go. Thanks for all your help. Let me know when you have something for me!"

I muttered a pointless goodbye. It was a waste of time. She was already out the door.

I felt dizzy as I killed the engine at the edge of the wooded park. After hearing about Raquel's new plan I needed some time to clear my mind. A few miles on Jacob's trails would do the trick. I pulled my shoes out of the trunk. I locked the car and hid the keys in the bushes. The wind picked up as I descended into the forest.

The fallen leaves now covered the protruding rocks and made navigating the path more difficult. They sloshed and crunched as they were crushed beneath my running shoes. The sun was setting, and it was getting colder, not enough for me to see my breath but the wind chill made me shiver. The woods were quiet. I pushed myself up another hill as the clammy shirt clung to my back. The wind moving through the trees spoke to me, in a ghostly voice.

"Lo siento."

I stopped. A deer jumped about fifty feet from the trail, hurrying up a bank and out of sight. So, I was hearing voices now? Had the nightmares manifested themselves in my waking reality? Was I slowly losing my mind? There was a sharp pain in my head. *Maybe you are just dehydrated*, I thought to myself.

I decided to take a break, sitting on a mossy log. The growth had turned yellow with the October frost and it smelled icily sweet. Sometimes when I ran, I imagined myself in the rainforests of Central America, desperately trying to escape the enemies my dreams manifested. What did "lo siento" mean? Was it a sign? I sat in silence, listening for the voices of the dead trees but there was nothing. It was getting cold. I walked back to the car. Maybe it was just all the stress getting the better of me.

12

The office was quiet the following day. I sat at my desk running programs that processed artwork. We had thrown the schedule out the window and I was still working overtime to try to catch up. The project was behaving like a corrupted file. Each time we ran a new process it splintered into multiple difficulties. Since the miscalculation in our planning we were even further off course. The management wanted results. With all the other projects I had going it was difficult to keep up.

I walked over to Jacob's cubicle to find some solace. Today I had brought him a gift. Folwell was getting rid of some of the library books they no longer needed, and I wanted to give him their copy of *The Count of Monte Cristo*. He looked over the colored illustrations. It was an old copy with detailed artwork accompanying the text. Along with the book I had brought him a bowl of vegetarian carrot soup I'd made for him.

"Don't worry, someday you'll escape," I joked.

"If I wanted to escape, I probably would have done so a long time ago."

"You know, Dantes was imprisoned with an old guy and used his burial cloth to get away after he died. Do you have a cloth for me?" I said, laughing a little.

"That's not funny," he smirked. "And what is in this Tupperware? Soup?"

"Yeah I made you some. You know, for your strength or something."

"Well, thank you. It's more than most would have done for me," he replied, setting the book and soup down on the desk and giving me a handshake.

"No problem. You're worth it."

He smirked as he picked up the book again and paged through it. I left him in his cubicle and returned to my own. For the other employees the day was almost over, but I still had a few more hours to log. Thirty minutes after everyone left Jon called me into his office and asked that I close the door behind me. His face looked solemn as he tried not to frown. He beckoned me into the chair opposite his desk.

"I'm sorry Daniel but I just don't think I can give you any more time. You have been such a good employee, but this work was supposed to be done months ago. I understand you have been through a lot, but that's not an excuse for this to be late."

"As additional problems piled up, I got a little sidetracked. I also helped the interns more than I probably should have."

They didn't deserve this, but I was in a corner.

"Our time is valuable, and I hate for you to waste it," he continued. "The department has decided to place you on probation."

"That's fair," I replied quickly.

"Listen, I don't want to do this to you, but I have no other options at this point."

"I understand," I replied.

There was nothing more to say as I quietly left his office.

I felt as though it was only an effort to break my will and make me more obedient. Was I being treated as a scapegoat for their own lack of progress? It was true that they had been behind since before I was hired. Because I couldn't make up the months they had lost, they decided to put the clamps on. Working slowly and throughout the evening, the automated computer formulas became buggy. As the night janitors began their routine the computer crashed. I stared at the blank screen and knew that this wasn't what I wanted.

"Fuck, fuck, fuck, fuck, fuck!" I pounded my fists on the desk. "FUCK!"

I slammed my hands on the keyboard and the "J" key popped off and bounced onto the floor. I picked it up and threw it over my cubicle wall, deep into the office.

"Dammit…" I slumped down into my chair.

What was I going to do without a job? Ruminate in fear over my Mexican dreams and forget my mind? I lost myself in calculations, desperately attempting to figure out where I had gone wrong. *I haven't gone wrong,* I told myself. *This fucked up world is what's wrong. I have done everything I possibly could to be good.*

"Fuck," I covered my face with the palms of my hands.

I began taking things off my desk and placing them in a brown paper bag. I couldn't stay any longer. My time was done, and the building was now letting me know that I could leave. I walked into my boss's open office and removed my grandmother's class ring from my necklace. I held it in my hand for a brief moment, examining the inscriptions. It was fashioned in an art deco style and as I gazed at it, I felt I could see back through the decades. It had begun its existence as a piece crafted by a skilled metal worker then, personalized with ownership, represented my grandmother's achievements. It had lingered in her jewelry box as a reminder of her time in school, finally becoming an heirloom by the default of an accumulation of years. Until recently it had signified the purpose of my being at the company. Now it seemed devalued in terms of sentimental value, becoming a symbol of corporate greed.

No one believed in these things anymore. After placing the ring on Jon's desk, I slowly turned away. Walking down the neat rows of cubicles I paused near Jacob's, feeling devastated by the sight of his empty chair. For a moment I wondered if he would understand when I didn't show up for work the next day or the day after that. I was tired of holding the world on my shoulders. It took me so long to realize that if we all held it up it would be a great deal lighter. I walked past the oversized rings and out the front door into the darkness of the frigid evening, alone and jobless.

13

Two and a half years prior, Felicia and I had stared up into the branches of a lone maple tree in the middle of a park. It seemed like ancient history after my time spent with Lacroix. Had it really been such a short time? The star shaped leaves could be mistaken for cannabis leaves were they not a startling scarlet. We let our fingers run through the soft grass as we lay on our backs, wondering where exactly life was taking us but not caring about it. Nothing mattered beyond the present moment. She and I had been dating for four months and treasured our walks through the glades of residential Saint Paul. We met while working at a drugstore. During a company function I had nervously approached and asked her out for a cup of coffee. It didn't take long for us to hit it off and soon we became inseparable, spending all our down time together. I didn't have a lot. I was a couple of years into a bachelor's degree and holding down multiple jobs. Some of the time was also spent working with the kids at the middle school, long before Raquel was hired.

Felicia was a first generation American. Her parents emigrated to the United States from Mexico before she was born. Now she lived in a tiny house near Cesar Chavez with about eight other relatives. The house seemed to be alive, taking in all those it came into contact with and exhaling the best smelling food you could imagine. Felicia had dark features, deep brown eyes and a golden complexion. She also had a curious looking birthmark under her left eye which made her all the cuter. The sun shone through the leaves and she shielded her eyes with one hand.

"Thanks again for helping us move," she looked over at me smiling.

"It's no problem. I'm happy to help."

In those days I owned a rusty old pickup that we would use to move their belongings. It was kind of an eyesore but more often than not got the job done. Felicia and I drove it into the ground taking our tours of the city.

"My mom will pay you in tamales, as usual."

Her mom's tamales were out of this world, the recipe a closely guarded secret.

"Alright, that sounds good. Will you pay me in kisses?"

I tickled her and she began laughing. We both sat up.

"Yeah, maybe. If you're lucky. Come on, let's go" she said, trying to pull me to my feet.

"Hey," I began as I stood up. "Be a chula, not a chola, Felicia."

"Watch out or i'll shave your eyebrows off and draw them back on with a magic marker. Then you will be a real chola!" She laughed. "I will always be the chula whether you like it or not!"

Her family had recently moved to Minnesota from Arizona to escape Felicia's abusive ex-husband. He had beaten her after a night of heavy drinking. She had disguised the incident as a car accident, until her family found out the car wasn't damaged. It wasn't long before she wandered to the Twin Cities and into my arms. Having been abused as a child it was easy for me to relate to her, though the psychic wounds her ex had inflicted were deep and slow to heal. I think she felt safe with me.

A little girl holding a stuffed bear opened the door. She looked sweet. Felicia's aunt ran a daycare for the other Latinos and the small space was sometimes filled with children. Felicia's uncle entered the room after her, wiping his hands with an old rag.

"Alright. So, what's first?" I asked him, looking eager.

The little girl scurried back across the room to a pile of toys.

"Well, pull your truck in back and my sons will begin stacking things into the bed. We will show you what you can help with after that."

His voice was hoarse with an odd articulation.

"Sure," I said, quickly doing an about-face back out to the pickup.

Felicia's uncle was a mechanic and loved fixing old cars. You could tell how hard he worked from the sweat lines on his shirt and the oil and grease under his fingernails. We worked through the afternoon carrying mattresses, coffee tables and boxes, neatly stacking them in the back of my truck. I would make the drive to Minneapolis several times that day, looking forward to the home cooked meal that would follow.

When the moving was done, we found ourselves sitting in a semicircle in front of the television on the living room floor. I pretended to understand the Spanish language television novellas, laughing about the characters' romantic entanglements. Felicia had me hooked and didn't have to force me to watch. The dramatic plot lines made for good conversation though they always ignored the fact that parts of Mexico were a war zone. At that time, I had just started reading about the drug violence there.

Felicia's mother spoke little English and after we had done the day's labor, dished us up. It seemed the cookware and dishes were the only things out of their boxes. I grinned as I stacked my plate high with tamales. I always felt spoiled on nights like this and her mom made sure I took some home in the plastic containers she had given me for such occasions.

The weeks passed and as we grew closer, I pictured our respective cultures intermingling. Her mother had become like a little piece of Mexico that Felicia had grown accustomed to. Every day she made the journey from her American job to her Mexican home, like a migrant worker passing over the border. The cultural difference gave Felicia doubts about where our relationship was headed but she told me that her mom had assured her I was a good catch. Today we were relaxing in Felicia's bedroom. Conveniently, her mom was downstairs doing laundry. We sat on the edge of the bed, Felicia with her head on my shoulder.

"What kind of future do you see for yourself, Daniel?" she asked.

"I don't know. Graduate from school, get a good job, settle down, have kids."

"Do you want to settle down with me?"

"Yeah, of course," I replied, putting my arm around her. She backed off a little.

"Are you sure I am what you want?" she pressed.

"Yes, you are," I kissed her forehead. "What kind of future do you want?"

"Well, I want to quit the job at the drugstore," she began. "I was thinking about signing up for classes at Saint Thomas."

"Isn't that a private school?"

"Yeah. Kind of expensive," she smiled anxiously.

"Well, I support you in whatever you want to do."

Felicia wrapped her arms around me and kissed me deeply. We fell back onto the bed. I ran my hand along the length of her thigh as she pulled me closer.

"What are you going to do now?" she teased.

"Mmm. I don't know. What do you want me to do?"

I kissed her again. The door handle began to rattle. Like two teenagers getting caught making out by a parent we quickly sat up. Our faces were flushed red and Felicia's hair was a little unkempt. Her mother entered the room with a load of laundry.

"Hola, Daniel. Cómo estás?"

"Ahh, bien!" I replied.

"Qué estaban haciendo ustedes dos aquí?"

I didn't quite understand what she was saying.

"Nada, mami," Felicia replied, her posture becoming rigid as she let out a nervous laugh.

"Nada?" Her mother looked me up and down. "Bueno."

Our sexual life was a taboo subject. Felicia's previous marriage had been an open relationship. She and her estranged husband would often welcome other people into their bed. When he became abusive all these developments were relayed to her mother in an effort to explain why he had abused her. It was no wonder why Felicia was not allowed to spend the night at my apartment. I understood that her mother was just being protective, but she was also not so quick to forgive.

"No bueno, mami."

Felicia stood up, gave her mom an unholy glare and stormed out of the room, slamming the door behind her. I looked at her mother, dumbfounded and shrugged my shoulders.

"Niña tonta," she looked up towards the ceiling, as if the phrase were some form of prayer.

I remained on the edge of the bed until she was done placing the folded-up laundry in the bureau.

"Be good, Daniel," she instructed as she left the room.

Suddenly I was alone.

The next day Felicia asked me out for a walk around her new neighborhood. We bought ice cream at a small cafe and continued down a staircase hidden in a forested area just off the road. We passed over a stream and under a low overpass, deciding on a nice grassy patch to sit down and rest. Felicia hugged her knees as I attempted to make small talk.

"It sure is nice out today," I said, breathing deeply.

"Yeah, I guess so..."

I turned to watch some people on the distant bicycle path. Felicia started crying. I sat shocked for a moment, before moving closer and putting my arms around her.

"What's wrong?"

"Daniel, I don't want you holding me. I asked you here because I wanted to talk to you."

I released her and braced myself.

"I slept with someone."

"What? What do you mean?"

"Someone came into the store and asked me out and I slept with him."

He had been a regular customer. He was another Latino who worked for a nearby construction company. Apparently, he had been flirting with her for a long time, asking her out again and again. Eventually she felt obligated to say yes. I supposed it was only a matter of time before our cultural differences took center stage.

"I cried when we slept together."

"What? Fuck, Felicia! I don't want to know. I don't want to know about any of it!"

"We can't keep seeing each other," she said, hiding her face in her hands.

We sat for several moments in complete silence as my mind screamed out, BITCH. BITCH. BITCH! repeatedly. I wanted to scream at her until my throat grew sore. I wanted to breathe fire.

"Daniel, walk me home, please."

Restraining my anger, I stood and helped her up, drying her tears with my hand as we walked awkwardly back to her house. What did I do to deserve this? The heartbreak was unbearable. Although I was well into my twenties, Felicia had been my first. That fact made it even worse. For a while I thought she had left me because I was balding or an inexperienced lover, but with time I realized it was because I didn't have something else, a basic understanding of their struggle and what it was to be Latino in the United States. As the nightmares began, I gained a sense of what she had been trying to tell me. She was living in another world. I had been so blissfully in love I hadn't even noticed.

In college I had been an ace, a star pupil with a near perfect grade point average. The breakup was the beginning of my downfall. After Felicia, everything changed. It felt like I could no longer show any emotion, I lived in constant fear of being hurt again. The love I had felt for Felicia was consumed by confusion and missed opportunities. I couldn't blame her for everything or escape the responsibility for my own actions. I was now stuck between unemployment and nightmares, searching the past for reasons why this was happening to me. Was it really all my fault?

There was no way she could have known how badly the end of our relationship would affect my mental health or that it would become the catalyst for my Mexican nightmares. I felt as though the tortured victims in my dreams wanted peace. How could I achieve that? If I took it all out on Felicia, was I really so different from the murderers in my nightmares? I felt like an animal, feral and wild. It seemed that something brewing deep beneath the surface was finally coming to a head for the first time. This raw sense of shame, this vulnerability, was now exposed. The tortured nights continued. The only difference now was that the pain in my nightmares was becoming a reality. I felt it.

14

I poured myself a cup of coffee, sitting down at my computer to begin the arduous task of editing my film. I wasn't sure if anyone would see it, but the video was all I had left. A lot of the narrative was meant to be inspirational but the parts about drug cartels, smuggling and drug violence were upsetting to me. Furthermore, I seemed to be the only one who cared or even paid attention. How was the situation supposed to improve if no one saw it that way I did? I had to change everyone's perspective. I tried to remain focused. I could still try to make a difference with my film from Saint Paul where it was safe. At least I wasn't in Mexico struggling with these thoughts.

What was I doing with my life? Everywhere I looked things were crumbling around me. I knew that I had to continue, that to become the person I wanted to be I might have to make more sacrifices. However, I was running out of things to give up. My apartment was all but bare and I could hardly afford to eat. Between looking for work and editing the film, I was exhausted. I clung to the hope my life would improve. I was ruminating about Mei almost constantly, inventing scenarios where she realized she had to have me. I fantasized that she was being held captive by the businessmen she worked for and that I would pluck her from the jaws of danger. I would, of course, become a famous filmmaker and use my newfound power and influence to protect her. "She would have no choice but to go with me," I imagined. "Who wouldn't?"

I had heard news that Mei had gotten a chance to take a vacation. She had gone to Portugal to bask in the sun. I was happy that she could get away for a while. She had earned it. But we were even further apart now; she was the cream floating on the top and I was sinking like a stone. Her world was all comfort and security whereas mine felt like a fight for survival in a city under siege.

I needed to find an interpreter to translate the film's narration for subtitles. I decided to email Raquel, considering she was one of the only people I knew who was fluent in Spanish. After sending her some sketches for her kids' party business I hadn't received a reply. I tried to contact Raquel again and again, begging for her assistance. It wasn't long before I received a phone call from the principal.

"I need you to stop contacting Raquel," she said abruptly.

I froze, a bitter taste in my mouth.

"My brother is a clinical psychiatrist and I think you might need to see someone like him," she continued. "You are a great guy, but you need to leave Raquel alone. Maybe you should just consider us friends at Folwell. We have enough volunteers for now."

"I don't know what you're talking about, really. I thought I was her friend," I replied, defending myself.

"She's been complaining about messages from you. She wants you to leave her alone," the principal said.

"She asked for my help with some projects," I tried to explain. "I was trying to find out what she thought about them and now she wants me to leave her alone?"

I felt a little destroyed. This was unwelcome news.

"I think it's your film. She wants to distance herself from it. She thinks your heart is in the right place, but you are not in a condition to market a film. I agree with her."

"She should be helping me," I nearly growled.

I imagined Raquel safely in her office. In my mind I saw her closing the door. I wanted to pound on it, begging her to open it again. I was reminded of Russ with my desire to force my way in. I immediately ended the thought, knowing it wasn't right. I had to let it go.

"Just stay away, okay? You have helped us a lot and we appreciate it. I'm sorry to say this but she is an employee and you are just a volunteer. In order to keep her happy, you need to go. She thinks you may be suffering from delusions of grandeur. You should get help."

"Yeah, thanks. Sounds like Raquel has been filling you full of bullshit" I snarled, hanging up.

It was discouraging. The principal had been paying me a little for some professional design work and the plug she pulled made my survival even more difficult. I didn't want to admit that I had a problem. Everyone had nightmares sometimes. Delusions of grandeur? There was nothing grand about what I was doing. I was running out of time and living on nothing. I had no choice but to keep moving. I knew a psychiatrist couldn't help me with this. I could find my own remedy.

I completed the film late one night and as I watched it for the first time, I finally felt some closure. My mind raced as I wasn't sure how to market and distribute it. There was potential here for new development and I wanted it to be positive.

I began sharing it with friends and relatives, even going as far as sharing it on Mei's social media wall in an attempt to show her that I had changed from my days doing drugs. I imagined her wondering, What is he doing? He had everything laid out before him and he threw it all away on a whim, following an impossible dream that arose out of a nightmare.

I thought of Marisol Garcia, the young criminal justice student who became sheriff of a violent Mexican border town. As the walls closed in around her, did she make a plan to escape with her family? Did she pack their suitcases in a state of heightened panic when the threats became too severe? I seemed to be following in her footsteps when I entered the bedroom, pulling my Mexican National Team jersey out of my dresser. I looked down at it, running my hand over the emblem of the eagle and the serpent in Tenochtitlan. This was clearly not my battle yet the nightmares, bearing their grisly warnings, had reached me all the way in Minnesota. I decided to get rid of the jersey once and for all.

Descending the back staircase, I walked out into the alley. As I neared the open dumpster a Latino man in a white rusted sedan pulled into the perpendicular intersection. It was as though a representative from the drug cartel had been sent to witness the display. I lifted the jersey into the air and threw it into the bin. I turned to walk away, feeling triumphant, as though a victory had just been won.

I went back up to my apartment and quickly packed a bag. Gliding down the front staircase I marched across the street to my car. I paused and looked over my shoulder as the rusted sedan crept slowly out of the alley and into my field of vision. The vehicle stopped and slowly reversed till it was hidden behind the building.

My heart skipped a beat. *What the fuck*? reverberated through my head. Had this been an actual threat, just a deja vu, or a misunderstanding? I opened the car door and sat in the driver's seat, catching my breath for a moment. I literally had nothing left, my sense of security now discarded along with my jersey. I buckled my seatbelt.

Driving away I thought of Marisol and her daring escape across the Mexican borderline, forever banished by a people she had fought so fiercely to protect. After she had made it to the United States the government had offered her no protection or support. Was this how those who took a stand were treated? My mind was too panicked to think. As I pulled onto the freeway I felt like a madman. I wanted to rewind my life, to make all these things go away. I didn't know what was real and what was imagined. I wanted to be a child again. I wanted to forget all this unholy hell. The next best thing would be to return to the place I had last felt safe. I would have to go home.

Daniel

15

I sped down Highway 52 through West Saint Paul, weaving in and out of traffic, my breathing rapid, my awareness heightened. I no longer felt safe in my apartment. I was considering the possibility that someone didn't like the film and had it in for me. I knew it was paranoid, but it was the only conclusion I could draw. Staying with my dad for the night was my only option. I had spent most of my early adult life with him, working the land as part of his small landscaping company. My family thought it was awful that I had been forced to leave my job. They had no idea of the extreme stress I was under.

Highway 50 was a rollercoaster of hills and I felt my stomach drop with each descent. Having made the journey hundreds of times, I knew each one intimately. After an hour on the road I entered my father's long driveway in a hidden corner of residential Red Wing. Dirt and gravel kicked up behind the car as it screeched to a halt in front of the old house. I pulled my bag out of the trunk and noticed my dad standing at the kitchen window with a puzzled look. I climbed the stairs to the porch and let myself in.

"What brings you home, Daniel?" he said, putting the dish he had been washing back into the sink.

"I just needed to get out of the city for a while."

"Is something wrong? You seem a little tense."

"It's about my film. I think some people were against it," I said nervously.

"I understand things must be hard for you after leaving your job," he said. "Why don't you sit down and rest for a while? It is probably all just a figment of your imagination."

"How do you know that?" I challenged.

"I just know," he replied, softly.

I eventually told my dad what had happened with the man in the sedan. His concerned look told me I could stay the night.

Dad was working feverishly as a small business owner, fighting a system that made making a profit nearly impossible. He was well regarded by many affluent members of the community, but he still toiled alongside his workers. Both of my parents had taught me the meaning of an honest day's work and had guided me with the insight to become a productive member of society.

That night I lay on the sofa drowsing fitfully. Suffering from insomnia, I was at the whim of my mind. Feeling defeated, I got up and went to the kitchen to warm up some chamomile tea. I began thinking about Mei while lingering under the light above the sink. I had her telephone number, though I never thought to call her. Maybe she hadn't liked my post on her wall. Or maybe she had forgotten about me and was busy being successful and important. I took a sip of tea and tried to picture what she might be doing. I ran through countless scenarios, putting her in places she would never have imagined for herself. However future events played out I was sure of one ending. She had to change her mind about me. I knew if she would only watch my film it would happen.

I imagined driving to the airport and waiting patiently by the baggage claim. Watching nervously across the sea of travelers, I would suddenly glance her face in the distance. She would stop short of me, about thirty feet away. We would be speechless. Suddenly she would run into my arms and give me a long passionate kiss. Perhaps if I became famous enough, they would erect a statue in the airport to immortalize the occasion. I sighed and went back to the couch, curling up and feeling sorry for myself. I so desperately wanted to find a way to meet her again.

In the morning I decided that I would just drive to Baltimore to see her. It wasn't something I had been planning but in the past few weeks I had made many hasty decisions. Driving across the country to see a girl you hardly even knew was considered crazy, but it might be my chance to win her.

I sent Mei a text message telling her I was coming and raced back out onto the main road. Speeding, I continued east into Wisconsin. I cruised through the farmland and small cities that dotted the countryside unstoppable on my journey to Baltimore, a place I had imagined my love story would truly begin. People just didn't do this shit. Why not though? *You only live once*, I told myself. We hadn't seen each other in seven years, and I had nothing left to lose. About two hours into the trip I received a call from Levi.

"What are you doing, man?" he asked. "Your dad called me and told me where you are going. Are you out of your mind?"

"Maybe. I don't know."

"Daniel, I don't know how to tell you this, but she has a boyfriend. I talked to her."

My heart sank.

"Yeah. I know she does…" I trailed off. "Well, I am going anyway. Maybe I can see some of the sights."

"You knew she had a boyfriend and you did this? What the hell, Daniel? I wouldn't go. Just leave it alone and turn back. She doesn't want you to come. If I had known your crush was this bad, I would have stopped you a long time ago."

"Why would you have stopped me?" I hissed.

The line fell silent.

"Just turn around, Daniel," Levi finally answered.

I argued with myself. I could go and profess my love to her and risk getting in a fight, or I could turn around and never see her again. I began to realize that this was reality. Women like Mei did not fall for guys like me. I couldn't say that I was going to lose her because I never had her to begin with. I continued driving, needing to make a decision and not yet having a reason to turn around. I screened phone calls from a distant area code I didn't recognize, not wanting to deal with what was happening on the other end. My dad finally called me half an hour later.

"Son, come back home. We can still talk about this."

"Dad, I think this is love and I may not get another chance. Don't you understand that? I really need to talk to her in person."

"Yes, I realize what you are going through, but she will be there tomorrow."

I didn't know what else to say.

"Daniel, you just quit your job and now you are chasing after this young woman? It seems very out of character for you. I know it is a little unwarranted but if you feel unstable you may want to consider checking yourself into a hospital. Maybe you just need someone to take care of you for a while. God knows I would if I weren't so busy with work" ," he continued.

I don't know what I expected. Something like the ending of a movie where she would change her mind and go with me. This wasn't Hollywood though. It was real life. My father was wise, and his advice meant something. Reluctantly I took the nearest exit to turn around.

Rochester, Minnesota had one of the biggest hospitals in the world. It was also in close proximity to Red Wing and the Twin Cities. I knew the doctors there might be able to help. Heartache was their specialty for wasn't love a kind of madness? They could fix my broken heart. This journey, I realized, had not been motivated by love, but by fear. I was running from something and it was about time I faced it. Who knows, I might have endangered Mei. What would I have done if I had gone there? I didn't even know which part of the city she lived in.

My drug use had prevented me from finding love, all those years spent in a narcotic-induced stupor were responsible for the state I was now in. *Russ must have had something to do with this*, I thought to myself, paranoid. *It's all his fault*! A sob escaped from my throat as I was reminded of my childhood. I tried to keep my eyes on the road. Why had this happened to me? Penniless, shattered and holding back tears, I was consumed alive by an unbearable sense of uncertainty.

16

I pulled into the hospital's parking ramp and grabbed the laptop bag from the back seat. After walking across the lot, the sliding doors opened, and I entered the emergency room. I hurried through the busy lobby to the front desk where an attendant sat shuffling papers.

"I am a filmmaker and I need to speak with a doctor and a policeman right away."

"What is your name, please?" the receptionist replied.

"My name is Daniel."

"...and you are a filmmaker?"

"Yeah, I guess. Sort of."

She looked confused.

"Why did you bring your film to a hospital?"

"Well, there are smart people here. I figured they would know what to do with it."

"And you also want a policeman? Why didn't you go to the police station?"

"I don't know. This is just where I ended up."

"Alright, well. We are going to admit you to a holding room so that a doctor can evaluate you. Please follow the nurse."

She nodded to a nurse in scrubs standing behind me.

"Don't worry. I don't think I'm Jesus," I said, laughing.

"I didn't think you were," the nurse replied.

"Apparently, I can't read minds either."

I spent an hour in the small holding room. I endured a barrage of questions from random doctors, then the nurse asked me to sit down in a wheelchair so he could take me to the psych ward. It wasn't long before I was all alone in a hospital room. It was large and had plenty of space to pace the floor if I felt so inclined. It had a single twin bed, a desk with a small light above it, a few cabinets where my possessions were locked away and a large pane of glass that looked out into a courtyard. The ward itself seemed sterile with white walls, white linoleum floors and drab looking beige curtains hanging on either side of the windows. There was a small nook with a television and a bookcase filled with random titles that patients could take at their leisure.

I was grateful that I didn't have to speak to anyone for a while. I felt mortified, suddenly seeing the situation from Mei's perspective. I tried to rest hoping that my attempt at a romantic gesture had not upset her too much. I decided to remain silent for as long as I could. The doctors came in and, writing them out on note cards, I tried to choose my words carefully.

I wrote: Please send Seal Team Six to guard my room and order some food. Then send it to Africa. They are starving.

I was sure the hospital workers had seen seven shades of crazy and I didn't like being one of them. I couldn't help blurting out the thoughts as they occurred. The doctors wanted to offer me a diagnosis and prescribe medication. It would help ease my symptoms, though I wondered what could be done about the stigma of having a mental illness. My vocal strike was about to end.

"Hello, Daniel. My name is Dr. Woods. How are you feeling?" His face was friendly.

Daniel

"You know, making these things red is probably not the best idea," I replied, looking down at the red paper hospital band on my wrist.

"And why is that?" the doctor inquired.

"It is on the wrist and red is like blood. Also, these barcodes kind of remind me of viruses. They are weird."

"Daniel, do you know what manic episodes are?"

I looked up from my wrist.

"They seem to describe themselves," I replied flatly.

"Yes. I think you've suffered a fairly large manic episode. We are tentatively diagnosing you with bipolar I disorder but we will revisit this after some observation. It will take nine months for a full recovery," he said, frowning.

"Are you telling me that I will need to stay here for nine months?"

He chuckled a little.

"No, but you will need to see a therapist and psychiatrist regularly and take prescribed medication. We don't want this to happen again."

"Yeah," I confessed. "Neither do I."

"I watched your movie and it was good. I just want you to do me one favor."

"What's that?"

"Don't think about starting any political action committees in the next nine months."

"I think I just want to stick with creative projects. I will leave that up to the politicians," I replied, now staring listlessly out the window. After a long moment I thought of something significant.

"Dr. Woods, have you ever had a client that kept thinking of Spanish words without knowing the meaning?"

He gave me a worried look.

"How do you mean? Are you hearing voices?"

"No, it happens in dreams. Sometimes in hallucinations. They are almost like daydreams."

91

"I see. No, I haven't heard of those particular circumstances, though stranger things have happened."

I looked back down at my wrist.

"Do you think it will affect my diagnosis?"

He paused.

"Patients who have manic episodes can experience a myriad of symptoms. I have a feeling your diagnosis will remain the same, at least while you are under my care."

"Thank you," I replied.

I reasoned with myself. I had done my best to change the world and it found me spending several days in a psychiatric ward. Was this what happened to people who tried to make a difference? Had I been sent here for reprogramming? I guess my bravery meant winding up in the hospital, not doing something great or changing things for the better. Not everyone could be a hero. Was I a villain? I didn't think so but at this point I wasn't sure.

The doctors asked me to fill out a crisis action plan and I did so with ease. Safe places to go in times of need were Fort Knox, Area 51 and the International Space Station. It asked what I could do if things got difficult and I wrote that I would call Mahmud Ahmadineyad, the President of Iran, and tell him to retire. I understood that the doctors wanted me to be serious about my recovery, but it hurt less to joke about it. Not being able to do much else, I sat on the bed for the rest of the day with my Michigan cap covering my eyes. My mouth twitched to a hint of a smile as I drifted off to sleep.

17

I walked down the hallway past numerous other patients and toward the common area. It was time for a group session, and they wanted me to get in on some discussions. I sat down next to a middle-aged woman in teal scrubs. There was a young man with shaggy hair and a hunch on his back with a Pink Floyd t-shirt sitting next to her. A teenage girl sat on the ground in a corner of the room with her head down and arms wrapped around her knees. Several more patients of varying age lined the perimeter, waiting for the group leader to speak. It was time to explain why I had come.

"Let's begin with introductions," the leader announced. "Say your name and one thing about yourself. It can be anything you want."

I was the first to go.

"My name is Daniel, and I came because I made a film. It's about Mexican drug violence and now I am here because I am afraid of the people causing it."

The shaggy looking patient spoke up.

"What if I were in the drug cartel? What would you do then?"

"Well, I suppose you would be kind of screwed since you are in a ward surrounded by doctors and security. Also, no harmful objects are allowed here."

"You don't think I could turn something here into a weapon?"

He leaned toward me a little. The group leader gave him a dirty look. I jumped back in my seat, suddenly feeling very vulnerable. My eyes begged the leader to say something.

"If you continue to make comments like that, we are going to have to place you in isolation," the leader scolded the man. "Don't threaten the other patients or your stay here may be longer than you originally planned."

"Whatever. I don't have to listen to you," he exclaimed defiantly. "After my seventy-two hours is up, I am out of here."

He gave me the stink eye and laughed. I tried to loosen my body a little, but my muscles remained twisted underneath my skin. There were a few other people in the group who were interested in what I was saying. They looked at me with curious eyes, thinking maybe I was up to something. It was a little ironic that I had wound up in a mental ward with patients sympathetic to drug dealers. Were these the people I was running from?

When it was time to eat the nurses distributed trays with our names on them randomly throughout the dining area. When I finally located mine, I found myself sitting across from a muscular man with olive skin and wild eyes. He cracked his knuckles, then his neck. I felt intimidated. He watched me squirm in my chair as two female patients appeared beside him, apparently ditching their seating assignments.

"You look kind of light on your feet. Are you sure you're not a ballerina?" he began, jokingly.

His smile was large and his glare intense. I nervously glanced around the room, looking for someone in authority. There was a nurse at the far end of the dining area. I began sending mental signals for assistance, but he must not have received them. He only turned and walked towards the nurses' station.

"I wouldn't mind. That would mean I would get to sleep with all the other ballerinas," I replied nervously.

94

He laughed.

"I have to say it. I heard from your buddy in the group. You have a lot of guts making a film like that."

Group sessions weren't mandatory. He obviously wasn't there. I would have noticed him. *Word gets around quickly here*, I thought.

"It's not a big deal. It is just about immigration. It also tells kids to say no to drugs," I returned.

"Well, isn't that a concept we can all get behind?" he said with a sarcastic laugh.

"Yeah. It should be anyway."

I stared down at my food. I could feel his eyes on me, dissecting me, trying to dig into my psyche.

"Come on, we are all friendly here. Don't be afraid to be who you are," one of the girls piped up.

We all stared at her, surprised. The man leaned back in his chair smirking and folding his arms. I suddenly felt like things weren't so bad.

"Well, I would like to see it someday," the man continued. "Say no to drugs. Hah!"

"It's really nothing," I stressed.

After lunch I walked back to my room and laid down on the bed, this time dreaming of Raquel walking with me, hand in hand, down the Colombian coast. At least she knew how to have fun, I thought. She also loved kids. When I tried to talk to Mei about them, she conveniently changed the subject. I sighed and pulled my hat over my eyes. Was I even mentally stable enough to have kids? I wondered. After an hour or so the doctor knocked lightly on the door.

"Daniel, do you mind if I come in?"

"Sure, " I replied.

"I am kind of confused as to why you came here. You said you were in love. Why didn't you keep going?" inquired Doctor Woods.

"Well, there was another dynamic to the situation. I had an encounter with a suspicious looking car in the alley behind my apartment. Afterward I went inside the apartment and prepared to leave. When I left it pulled out into view and when I turned to look it slowly slunk back into the alley. I wasn't feeling very safe so traveling cross-country was probably not the best idea."

"I see. Do you still think you are in danger?"

"No. I'm not sure if I ever was. Does it seem like a legitimate threat to my wellbeing?"

"I can't say."

"That means that it might have been, I guess. I am just happy to be safe now," I said, stretching.

"Yes. That is a good thing."

"My fear backed me into a corner," I frowned. "I just need to figure out how to get out of it."

"We would love to help you do that," the doctor smiled.

After the conversation I went into the cafeteria and played Apples to Apples with the shaggy patient from group, the intense man and the girls from lunch. I had never played the game before and thought it was kind of funny, considering the circumstances. We laughed and talked for a while, forgetting we were in a psychiatric ward. Everything had gone crazy and for now I took comfort knowing I was being cared for. Afterward I grabbed a few books and brought them into my room.

I read under the glow of a neon light above my bed. It created a slow hum, a kind of electric tranquility. I was still alone though the doctors had indeed mended my heart. For the first time in months I was not obsessing over Mei. Perhaps I could close the door on that particular part of my life. Here, in this place, I felt like it was possible. I would be ready for another adventure soon.

18

I dart between trees, avoiding roots, pushing through dense foliage with greenery in my face. I am sweating and panting. Peering through some thick growth on the side of a tree trunk I spot another man dressed in camouflaged Kevlar of the Mexican armed forces. It is Levi. He is brandishing a heavy automatic weapon. I motion to him with a hand signal and we continue stalking our prey through the thick tangled vines. In the distance stands a secluded mansion patrolled by men with assault rifles. I think "The nightmares are finally over," but, in the moments that follow, the flurry of gunfire blows my mind and lays waste to any sense of comfort. I throw myself to the ground. I am winded, I can't breathe, and the shots are deafening.

My breaths were quick and uneven. My chest heaved and I could feel a dull throbbing within. I sat up in bed and placed my hand on my sternum. My stomach felt like a muddy pit into which a rock had been thrown. The stone had hit the bottom with a thud as grime splattered everywhere. I went down the dimly lit hallway to find the night nurses. They sat behind a desk watching a wall-mounted television near the nurses' station. There was nothing good on, nothing ever is at four in the morning. Shuffling across the floor I felt like a child who had just woken and wandered into his parents' bedroom after having a bad dream. Were the good guys in charge of my nightmares now? I had heard the Mexican army was corrupt so perhaps not.

"Do I have anything prescribed to help me sleep?" I asked the nurse.

"Let me check. Hold on."

He turned the volume down on the television and went for the desktop computer. After a minute or two of scrolling he replied.

"Sorry, you don't have any sleep meds. I can get you some tea. Sometimes that helps me when I can't sleep."

"Alright. That sounds good. I do that too when I am at home."

Looking for drugs to sleep. I had never needed them before. Why did I think I needed drugs now? I wandered off to bed feeling disenchanted. I still couldn't fall asleep, so I left the light on with my face hidden under my hat. When I tipped up the cap a few hours later there stood Levi at the door to the hospital room.

He seemed apprehensive as he approached the bed, sitting down in the chair next to it. No one really knew what to do when things like this happened. It was embarrassing for everyone involved. Only Mei could really confirm whether or not she even had an interest in me. Levi was here to tell me that she didn't.

"So, you're here to tell me you've sided with her boyfriend?"

"It's not like that, Daniel. She gets to decide who she dates, not you."

"Did you even stick up for me?"

There was a slight pause.

"I didn't need to. She doesn't feel the same way about you."

I was caught feeling ashamed of my friend. Why hadn't he fought in my corner? To him it obviously didn't matter if I loved her or not. It was much easier to tell himself that I didn't. I couldn't understand why he was acting that way. I felt betrayed, which might not have bothered me if he had been friends with her, but he was *my* friend, he was supposed to have *my* back. It felt like he was trying to talk his way out of our friendship. I was trying to decide if I cared any more as he changed the subject.

"How is your family doing? Have they been here to visit you?" he asked.

"Yeah, my mom and dad have," I conceded.

"What did your mom say?"

"Not much. Just that she misses me, and she wants me to visit her soon."

My mom and I had grown close in my adult life. I called her often but seldom went to visit her. I think she felt guilty about what had happened between Russ and I as kids and ashamed that she was unable to put an end to it. Now she only watched me from afar, often helpless to offer the support I so desperately needed from her. Levi had known her well from our time as adolescents.

"The bipolar thing can be unpredictable if it isn't treated," he continued.

I really didn't want to hear this.

"Yeah, I will have to be more careful next time. That's all."

"I really don't like seeing you get your heart broken."

I frowned.

"You haven't done much to prevent it from happening."

"What do you want me to do? Force her to talk to you?" he snapped back.

"No," I said, withdrawing a little.

"That's what I thought."

We sat like this for several moments as I thought about the reason for his visit. Of course, he considered himself a good friend and cared about my wellbeing, but why was it so hard for him to acknowledge the validity of my feelings? I couldn't figure it out.

I suspected he was politically jockeying for position. Staying on Mei's good side might grant him certain opportunities and reeling me in could potentially be seen as a favor to her. I was speculating, sure, but wanted no part in any of it. Technically he was there to support me. I'd have to leave it at that.

He started to stand up.

"You don't have to go. I just need you in my corner."

"Do you realize how badly you freaked her out?"

"Yeah, I guess I would be freaked out too." I frowned. "Listen, I don't want you to have come here for nothing, but I don't have a lot to say."

"I can just sit here for a while if you want," he replied, leaning back in the chair.

"That's fine."

"I'm sorry things didn't work out for you, or for us really. I don't need your help with Detroit anymore. I think I have it under control."

The displeasure in his acknowledgement was apparent.

"Oh…" was all I could muster.

"Don't take it personally. It has nothing to do with this Mei business."

"I'm sure it doesn't," I replied, sarcastically

"It doesn't. I said don't take it personally. There just isn't enough money. I might just have to cancel it. It is going nowhere."

"A lot of things seem to be going nowhere these days."

Levi looked concerned but didn't immediately reply.

I felt lost, as though an important piece of me had been severed from my body. In my mind I was desperately trying to find it so it could be reattached. Was the end of the Detroit project a grim metaphor for the end of our friendship? I didn't know how to respond. I wanted Levi and I to remain close but it seemed that my attraction to Mei had caused a deep schism between us. He lingered for a while but decided to leave within fifteen minutes. I felt devastated by his absence.

Later that afternoon I gathered all my possessions and put them into a paper bag. When the doctor let himself into the room I was standing at the window, looking out into the courtyard.

"I know you want to leave but I need you to stay a few more days for observation," the doctor began.

I turned to face him, trying to assert myself.

"I understand that, but I have things to do. I need to make money," I replied.

"You will be healthier if you stay. I would hate to see this happen to you again," he cautioned.

"My family is in debt and so am I. Work is important to me right now." I continued, "I need to be able to support myself."

"Well, you are leaving against my orders then," he insisted.

"Yes, I suppose I am," I said, latching the flap on the bag. "Can you have someone open this other cabinet so I can get my jacket and my laptop out?"

I walked off the ward and through the long hallways and corridors of the hospital.

I exited through the same sliding glass doors I had entered days before, my bag slung over my shoulder. Driving through rural Minnesota, I headed back to my hometown, ready to dust myself off and start over again. I was lucky to have a job and a future with my family waiting for me there.

I was eighty thousand dollars in debt, and I knew my story wasn't a fairytale. It was time to start chipping away, returning to work the land from solid bedrock. I had plans that needed to be seen through. I knew that someday the culmination of my struggles would mean that I could once again sleep soundly. No matter what happened going forward, I would always have my film. That would have to do.

Part Two

19

I spent the next month sleeping fitfully on my grandmother's couch. My dream was over. I had no real home anymore; this was as near to a place of my own as I could get for now. "For now," was exactly the length I was told I could stay. Dawn filtered through the half-drawn curtain as I stretched my aching body over the armrest. I ran my hand across a stubbled cheek and groaned as I lifted myself off the sofa. Staring groggily out the window, the frost on the lawn seemed to glimmer. I couldn't help but think of Mei, still half a continent away. The thought, like the ice on the blades outside, would disappear with the approaching sunlight. After a moment of helplessness, I walked into the kitchen to pour myself some juice. These mornings were slow and cold. I didn't know which was worse, the creaks in that old house or those in my weary body. I grabbed a piece of pastry off the counter. I put my boots on and headed out to work.

As I exited the house thoughts of Mei still plagued me. Frozen mud from my dirty boots, which had been left outside overnight, crumbled on the ground as I walked. Reality took hold. Those thoughts could wait for lonelier, less productive moments. I made my way in my aging car to our shed, and upon arrival I began loading a rusty old one-ton truck.

My father had spent the last several years landscaping the Red Wing Historical Society, a garden he designed to mimic the native prairie of the region. I smiled as I drove the beat-up one-ton along the city's waking streets.

I pulled the weed whip from the truck and began threading the cord. The grasses were still tall from the previous fall and needed to be cut. I fumbled with the components as my hands froze in the March air. After everything was in place, I pulled the starter and began to work. The whip had a special meditative quality. The vibrations it sent through my body set my mind into a false sense of security, at odds with the deafening sound it produced. It was as though the sound and vibration put me into a place outside of time. When I closed my eyes after going to bed at night, I still seemed to be cutting the grasses on the back of my eyelids.

The area was still dead from an unseasonably cold winter though there were small signs of life appearing everywhere, buds on the trees, crocuses poking up through the frozen earth. The birds had returned weeks ago and were busy making nests out of the brush I created. For a while I had become instrumental in the cycle of life.

The museum was mostly the private collection of a titan of American industry who had made millions in this sleepy little village. The area held an atmosphere of quiet dignity.

I continued working through the afternoon as I crisscrossed the garden, every now and then dragging tarps filled with debris into the truck. My favorite thing about the one-ton was that the bed had a lift. My father's employees spent hot summer days having races up its bed at full tilt. I had more happy memories of that truck than many of my old friends. When the bed was filled with trimmings, I would take it to a local farm, dodging geese and goats as I maneuvered to the brush pile. As soon as I returned, I kept pushing the whip, creating a tide receding into the ocean of grass, the melting snow bringing life to the small stalks and seedlings below.

106

The end of the day approached, and my father came to the job site. The man looked hardened, with thinning gray hair and serious but confident eyes. After years alone, captaining a failing business, he knew what hardship was. Feeding me on Ayn Rand and Frank Lloyd Wright had been one of his passions and now, old enough to appreciate it, I was thankful for the depth he added to my life.

I laughed a bit, imagining what I seemed like, stoned, walking from class to class carrying a thick copy of Atlas Shrugged. I admired the characters in the book, and to me, my dad was like one of them, a silent figure with a passion and eye for design that few could match. His installations seemed to rise out of the ground as if carved out by a glacier. They looked so much more natural than the generic paving stones and decorative rock most favored. While others bordered their houses with man-made divisions, we were carving waterfalls out of hillsides. For a hefty price you could hire us, though it was a shame my father's skill in crafting the ground didn't translate into business sense. The budget was tight, and we weren't always paid on time.

"I need some company. Come with me to the hardware store," he said.

He was wearing a dirt-stained denim jacket with a pair of old, ragged work pants. His wiry hair stuck out from underneath a weathered cap.

"Sure thing," I replied.

I threw the whip in the back of the truck and jumped in his car. We didn't say a word as we pulled into the hardware store parking lot. Jumping out almost immediately, I hesitated by the door for a moment until I could follow him in. We were after parts for fountain pumps and as he checked the threads on the links, I pretended to be interested in the long wall of boring plumbing equipment. It was not the most exciting job, but I loved the outdoors and I loved my dad. He found what he needed and like a little duck I followed him back to the counter. He paid the man and drove me back to the Historical Society. I didn't know why he brought me along. I think he wanted some time with his son, though we hadn't said anything. He parked, let the engine idle and turned to face me.

"Do you really want to work for me for the rest of your life?" he asked.

He clearly thought I was wasting my time, though he desperately needed reliable workers.

"I don't mind working for you and I am still looking for additional design work."

We had this conversation sometimes. I was not a prodigy by any standard but good enough to make a living. I think it was confusing for him because I didn't want what most of his employees wanted. Instead of heading to the bars after work I spent my time tinkering on my film.

"…and you're happy with that?"

"Yeah." I said quietly.

"How are you feeling, you know, mentally? Are you okay?"

"Yes, Dad," I gnarled through my teeth.

"Good."

"Just don't ask," I continued. "I will tell you if something is wrong."

"Alright, Daniel," he paused. "This year is going to be better, okay? No more screwing around. We are going to make a profit," he assured me.

This conversation happened more frequently than actually making a profit.

I smirked, "I know we are, Dad."

If this year was going to be different I had yet to see any signs of change. Light rain began to fall as I headed back to the shed, the sun's warmth gone and its light now fading behind a mass of gray clouds. I was now facing another cold, lonesome night. At least my grandma was waiting for my return. It felt nice to have someone waiting for me, but it also reminded me that soon I would be back to living alone, back to the pain of isolation, back to life without Mei, back to life without anyone. Maybe that wasn't completely true, but I definitely felt like it was.

20

Mei walks through the dusty streets of Tijuana wearing a pretty flower-print sundress. She stops in the middle of a vacant street and looks up into the sky, as though she was becoming lost in something beautiful. A light wind blows, and her hair seems to be floating in the breeze. Suddenly an alarm goes off. Gunshots pierce the air. A nearby storefront shatters and shards of glass are cast out into the street. Bullet-holes can be seen appearing one by one in a building on the opposite side of the street. They near closer and closer to Mei. She screams.

"Get down!" I yell, tackling her to the ground.

We go down to the cement with a dull thud. I lay on top of her, protecting her from the violence happening several yards away. A car speeds around a corner. You can hear tires squealing in the distance. The noise gets closer and closer until the car speeds past, nearly running us over as we lay on the ground.

"Entra! Entra!" the driver yells.

Three men emerge from the building carrying large canvas duffle-bags. They all pile into the car and pull away. Two squad cars whip around the corner and speed after them in pursuit. I look down at Mei to see if she is alright and all I see is a sack of potatoes. The small boy from the food stand in Cesar Chavez walks by.

"Wow! You really fell for her, señor," he snickers.

I woke up, laughing. What the hell was that? A sack of potatoes? My subconscious was being a smart ass apparently. The room was still dark but the sky outside turned to shimmering pastels as the sun rose. I reached over to the nightstand to see what time it was. My alarm clock was missing. It was then that I realized I was in my own bed in the Twin cities. I had driven to my old apartment to pack my belongings for the move to a new apartment in Red Wing. I stretched, pulled the blankets off and wandered into the bathroom to do my morning routine. Levi would be coming to help me move today.

Mid-morning, I glanced down at the street from the apartment window and noticed Levi exiting his car and making his way toward the building. As youths we probably had more fun than we should have had. If only we had kept some of that innocence. He reminded me of Mei now and it made me bitter. He was trying to rebuild our friendship though, so I decided to give him a chance. We talked as I packed, and he swept up the floor.

"I feel like I am leaving a piece of Mei here," I sighed.

"Get over it. She has never even been here, man," he replied.

"Yeah. I realize that. I guess it is just leaving the city."

"She doesn't even live here!" he exclaimed.

"Well, Baltimore and Saint Paul are both big cities, right?"

"You are hopeless," he sighed.

I sighed as well and placed another plate in the box. I felt foolish obsessing over her still, but it felt like a big loss. I tried not to let it get the best of me as I wrapped another plate in paper towels. Frowning, I thought about how fun it would have been to have the four of us together. I imagine Levi and Anna had seen a woman of a much higher status. I also saw her as somewhat unattainable, but I was still angry because they had not supported me in my romantic pursuit. I suppose I could have been a little more tactful about it.

We talked more about old times, hanging out in a friend's basement and experimenting with mind altering substances. I hated talking about it but Levi considered it one of the most liberating experiences of his life. So many wasted nights there while Mei and Anna were safe at home studying. Why hadn't I been more like that, and if I had been, would I still be thinking of her today? I put several more dishes in the box, placing paper towels in between. Levi called into the kitchen from the next room.

"Do you want to go for a walk? I have to pick up some mail."

"Let's try to finish up some of this stuff first," I responded.

"Are you alright, Daniel? I mean, do you need to talk about this? You seem distracted. You hardly even knew her, right?"

"No. You are right. I have to move on," I conceded.

"Don't worry, man. I'm sure there will be others."

"Thanks," I replied, duct taping the box closed.

"Let me give you some advice, something I have learned over time. You need more than love if you want things to work."

"You really think that is true?" I sounded skeptical.

"Yeah, I know it is true."

I shook my head. There was something inherently wrong with that statement. Surely love was enough. Wasn't it?

I put on my jacket. It had the word "Camel" stitched on the back, though it wasn't advertising cigarettes. I had bought it in Chinatown in Los Angeles before I got my job at Lacroix and it was obviously designed to emulate American culture. It bothered me a little but not enough to get rid of it. I figured it reminded me to stand up straight so I wouldn't get a hump. Ever since I was young clothes had been an integral part of my identity. I didn't necessarily need any named brand but symbols like my Michigan hat were important to me. I wanted what I wore to say something about who I was but also have a special meaning that no one could understand but me. The memory of traveling to Los Angeles with my family was also important and it felt like a warm hug from them to wear the coat.

We drove across town to Grand Avenue, a busy shopping district tucked away in residential Saint Paul. I peered into every shop window as we walked. Levi told me about his children's latest exploits.

"Julian is struggling in school. We are really trying to prepare him for higher level classes in middle school, but he just isn't understanding certain things," Levi confided.

"Really? I guess I thought he would have been doing better. You and Anna are so good about teaching him things."

"Hah. Maybe life lessons, but math and spelling are different stories all together."

"I see..." After a slight pause I continued. "I remember when we met at the beginning of middle school. I think at that point we were both doing pretty well. Hopefully he will pick up again and follow in your footsteps."

Levi chuckled.

"Hopefully he won't inherit my crazy anxiety. Man, I hated that time in my life. It was so awkward."

"You know, I actually really treasure those times," I admitted. "I look back at middle school and I really liked myself then. I can't say the same for later in life."

"We really were better versions of ourselves."

"Do you remember when I bought those oversized shoes? I really wanted this style and I could only afford the sale item that was oversized. You called me Bobo the clown."

Levi laughed louder.

"How could I forget Bobo the clown?"

"And then I drew a picture of you as Bigfoot in my notebook and gave you Groucho Marx eyebrows."

"Hey, don't make fun of my caterpillars," Levi raised his eyebrows.

"And your hairy hobbit feet."

114

"Ugh, don't remind me."

I ran my hand over my bald head.

"Things have changed a lot since then," I lamented.

"They sure have. I am glad we are still friends though."

"Surprisingly," I muttered a little, suddenly forgetting the good memories the conversation had instilled in me.

Levi gave me a funny look and we continued walking. His face became solemn.

"One of my strongest memories of you was when we were in middle school. I was at your house and your brother was abusing you."

"That's why no one ever came to my house."

"He was beating you up and then he turned and looked at me as though I was next. It scared the shit out of me."

"That's how I felt every day."

I was heartbroken remembering this.

"How did you get through life never mentioning that to anyone?"

"I just didn't want to complain," I replied.

"Well, with your life, I feel like you should complain more."

I looked down at the ground and scraped one of my shoes against the pavement as we walked.

"I don't want to complain," I mumbled, stopping to stare at myself in the reflection of an empty storefront. Balled up fists tightened at my sides as I caught a glimpse of Levi standing next to me. Anger welled up in me as I remembered Russ. I felt my dilemmas with Mei and Levi were mere extensions of what he had done.

"I worry about you, Daniel."

"Don't. I am fine," I snarled back.

"Alright," Levi backed off. "It's your life, man."

Levi picked up his mail. I remained silent as he thumbed through the envelopes. He asked the postman if any packages had arrived for him today. There weren't any. We exited the store and crossed the street into some of the quieter parts of the neighborhood.

"I used to feel like I was going to be an addict, man. I thought it was a part of who I was. Now that I have a family, I really have to face the music about my past. Sometimes I get the urge to use drugs again," Levi admitted.

"If you think you are an addict, you enable yourself to become one," I replied.

"Good point. I will think about that."

Despite Levi's attempt at newfound support, I was growing bitter. Addiction was something I was trying to avoid, and I feared his desire to use drugs had become an all-consuming evil. Levi had sometimes acted as my impromptu therapist but in this moment his own vices seemed to poison his wisdom. I understood his thoughts on the issue, but it was a risk I no longer wanted to take.

Levi drove us back to my apartment. We lingered outside.

"Can you keep helping or are you going to take off?" I asked, secretly wanting him to leave.

"I need to look after the kids. Anna has somewhere to be so…" His eyes looked into the distance.

"That's fine. I can finish up," I replied, relieved.

"Listen. Don't worry so much about Mei. You will find someone even better. There are other fish in the sea."

"Easy for you to say. You are married."

"You know what I mean."

"Yeah, yeah," I turned and left Levi standing on the boulevard.

"See you later, Daniel!" he yelled back at me.

I raised my hand as I disappeared into the apartment building.

I somberly climbed the staircase to my third-floor apartment. My anger faded. I strolled through the now empty space with my hand caressing my cheek. The time to think of her should have passed and I understood it would be healthier to focus my attention elsewhere. I knew other women would play a part in my future as I ran my finger across a dusty windowsill. I didn't want to let go. I positioned the

116

memory of her in a safe corner of my mind, as though protecting it from something unseen. Now I was starting a new adventure without a heroine. I didn't know exactly what lay ahead, only that I would be facing it alone. As I closed the final box and taped it up, I turned to the window and filled the emptiness with the only thing I had left. Uttering one last phrase into the glass, leaving the feeling in the pane for someone else, I whispered, "Love for Mei…"

Grabbing my jacket, I walked across the hardwood floor with heavy steps, headed for the door. The sound of it closing echoed through the empty apartment. I turned the key in the lock and left for a new life back home.

Daniel

21

I drove half an hour south to a Cambodian Buddhist temple I remembered seeing as a child in the farmland just south of Saint Paul. Interested in learning more about meditation practice, I decided spirituality was what I needed to start over.

I had called in advance to speak to a monk. I knocked on the door and a young boy appeared, welcoming me. He smiled and had me wait in an ornate room with interesting golden hued wallpaper. Someone in an adjacent room was speaking on the telephone in what I assumed was Cambodian.

After a few awkward moments the monk appeared, wearing the traditional orange robes of the Theravada. He was a young man in his twenties, probably about the same age as me with a shaved head and calm features. I was sure they sent him because he was more accustomed to western culture. It must have seemed strange because outsiders to this small community were so few and far between. I didn't understand exactly what I was looking for though I thought he might be able to point me in the right direction.

I began, "I have a deep-seated passion to make a difference in the world. I have always been interested in Buddhism and I feel like learning more about the beliefs could help me become a better person. I have never taken the time to formally speak with someone about it. I am not sure if this is the correct understanding, but I feel it has a type of diplomacy attached. To me Buddhists are like the glue that holds the world together. They are here making things peaceful, life after life."

"That statement is somewhat true," he replied, "but we have little to do with politics. The Theravada have no figurehead like the Mahayana's Dalai Lama, and are usually found in countries like Cambodia in Southeast Asia. You should come back in a week or so when we will all gather to experience Theravada Buddhism. I want you to meet a member of our board of directors, a lay Buddhist. He will be better at explaining these things in proper context."

"Yes, I would like that," I agreed.

After I spoke a little more on my life, he excused himself. I thanked him for his time and climbed back into my vehicle, heading back to the highway and my grandmother's couch.

Returning a week later, I bypassed the house where the monks lived and drove further up the hill to an elaborately decorated building. The architecture was impressive with intricately carved bannisters, grand staircases and a gold peaked roof. I thought it curious that the structure was surrounded by serpent statues. These creatures were the Buddhist guardians of knowledge, a similarity between Buddhism and Christianity's garden of Eden. I stepped through one of the lower doors and carefully removed my tennis shoes. Entering a room covered with murals in vibrant greens, oranges and blues, I noticed a far wall surrounded by Buddha statues. I was early but already noticed I was the only non-Cambodian there. It was strange to be mingling in the smartly dressed audience with my faded Wolverines cap and old jeans. At least I had worn a sweater.

The man I was supposed to meet signaled me from across the room to come and talk with him. Though I didn't know what he looked like, he was the only one paying any attention to me. He was an older, short, balding man with tortoiseshell rimmed glasses. He started with a lesson in precepts, the five Buddhist commandments for lay people.

"These are the Buddhist precepts by which you must abide," he informed me.

> Do not harm living beings.
> Do not take things not freely given.
> Do not commit sexual misconduct.
> Do not commit false speech.
> Refrain from using intoxicants.

It was clear that many of these rules were like the Ten Commandments and there were more depending on your level of devotion. These were the most basic. He told me more about the life and times of the Buddha, a Hindu prince who became a sort of prophet after realizing life's impermanence and seeking an end to human suffering.

Soon the ceremony began, and we walked in a circle holding candles and saying mantras that I could not understand. I kept my mouth shut and lost myself in the vibrations. Afterward we were seated, and the monks spoke for a very long time. I can only imagine that they were expounding some ancient wisdom. Smiling, I tried to listen, for what I'm not sure. They did not have a specific leader, but one monk did sit above the others on a high throne. The younger monk from earlier was also in attendance and held a small sheepish smirk. I occasionally glanced at the murals that surrounded us, telling the story of the Hindu prince. With no explanation I could only imagine the meaning.

After two hours the speeches ended, and I was invited to a bowl of delicious soup prepared by the lay people. The monks could not eat anything after noon, though it was customary for the members to bring them offerings of food. I slurped it up gratefully as the board member told me about a stupa, or monument, they were erecting in the Buddha's honor that would house a bone from his finger. I thought it was interesting but a little eerie for them to have a relic like that in the Midwest. Most countries in Asia would be humbled to have something so profound. It would be similar to a Christian church in Cambodia inheriting a piece of the Shroud of Turin. You can imagine what an honor it was for them to have it.

I learned a lot from this man. His presence was comforting, and I thanked him for his kindness. I wished him well, quietly ducking out and dodging glances from a few curious Cambodians. The experience had been a positive one, and as I rolled back out onto the road, I experienced a fleeting moment of happiness.

On the way back to Red Wing I stopped in Miesville to fill my tank. Miesville was a tiny farming community with a population as scant as the amount of money dwindling in my bank account. Zipping up my coat I placed my hands in my pockets and turned my back to protect myself from the wind. Growing resentful of the church, I was also turning my back on my upbringing. I didn't know what else to do. Light flurries graced my cap and the shoulders of my jacket. I felt like one myself, being aimlessly thrown in whichever direction the wind was blowing.

On the way home I stopped at the grocery store to buy some ingredients for making chili. As soon as I got inside my apartment my cat greeted me. I navigated around furniture and unpacked boxes, placing the groceries on the kitchen counter. I pulled my cutting board out of a box. The flat piece of wood was a familiar sight. I faced it down on the counter and began to cut peppers for the chili. The onions would be next, though I already had tears in my eyes. These fake tears became real. I promised myself that things would get easier.

22

Our next jobsite was one we simply called "the valley." The valley was located somewhere in rural Wisconsin. A man lived there who was a client of my father's and it was my job to cut stone for him with a twenty-inch diamond-tipped blade. The massive pieces of flagstone sometimes weighed over one hundred pounds and the water of the saw was like liquid ice. Anyone would become hardened doing this kind of work.

I waited every day for the sun to rise above the barn and warm me. When your hands are numb, and you are working with water and spinning steel you tend to appreciate any source of warmth that you can find. Zeke, the hired man working alongside me, made life interesting, and our two saws were deafening in the cool spring air. These days were long and painful. I tried not to think, instead letting the flying bits of limestone become my inner dialogue.

Zeke was tattooed, full of cynicism, and completely paranoid about corporate America. He thought that FARC rebels in Columbia were guarding bananas and cocoa for the produce and candy companies. These militias were hell bent on dominating the locals, supposedly bending them to their sweet and delicious wills. Banana plantation Nazis were a regular topic of discussion on this job site. Zeke was more of a roughhouser who had cut his eyebrow open on a broken bottle in a bar fight. There was now a massive scar above his right eye. Feeling a little cocky one morning he affectionately dubbed me "Buttercup" and I shot back at him with "'Morning Glory." Today was no different. The banter continued.

"Do you know why they can't find the Yeti?"

"No, Zeke, I don't," I said, laughing a little.

"I saw a video of one teleporting."

I stared at him in disbelief but flat out gut-laughing now.

"I might actually believe that one," I replied, still laughing.

Our lives were simple but difficult. We were each burdened by debt to others and this played constantly on our minds. Some may have called Zeke a criminal or a vagrant, though I knew his hard work was supporting his family. Despite his patchwork history it seemed he was endlessly trying to straighten out his life. Our banter, mostly inane, aimed to hide the fact that our bodies shouldered the heavy burden of supporting an ailing company. We were grateful for it. Because of the failing economy, even work like this was hard to come by in a town as small as Red Wing.

We had both seen our share of hardship and we had each narrowly escaped death. He and I spent time on topics most would consider unbelievable, like metaphysics and alternate realities. Even though he identified himself as Christian he would sometimes hear out the bits I had learned about Buddhism. No topic was off limits as we traded barbs about drug use and relationships gone bad. On many points we agreed to disagree. Zeke made me rethink my stance on my drug conversation with Levi. It was clear to me that drugs scattered the mind and took it places it would not normally wander. For Zeke that was a good thing.

His smile suddenly faded as his mind ran over a wound from long ago.

"I was involved in a car crash once. My friend had taken some LSD and we decided to go for a ride. He was driving too fast and before I knew it, we were headed right for a light post. It was a fight or flight moment and if I had been wearing my seatbelt, I never would have been able to jump from the vehicle."

"How fast were you going?" I asked, feeling a little tense.

"Oh, I don't know, about seventy."

"Wow. I would think you would have died jumping out of a car at that speed."

"Well, actually, I was wearing a leather jacket which took most of the beating," he confided. "After that my friend wasn't the same. He got brain damage from the crash and we would visit him in the hospital. We even snuck him out a couple of times to smoke grass, but he never fully recovered. He eventually killed himself by overdosing on his medication. He just couldn't handle living like that."

I had heard too many stories like this one. Anyone who did a lot of drugs and didn't having a story like that to tell was fortunate. I felt sorry for Zeke because he had experienced so much trouble. We were like kindred spirits and though I didn't completely agree with his stance on drugs, I respected his right to do what he wanted to do with his own body. Free will follows its own whims. I never thought I would end up doing drugs when I was little, but I started doing them all the same.

"I understand. That must have been rough." I confided, "I have had trouble with drugs in the past. I smoked a lot of pot in high school and I tried cocaine a few times. I did a lot of prescription pain medication and even overdosed on mushrooms."

"I didn't know you could overdose on mushrooms," Zeke sounded surprised. "You seem like a pretty smooth operator though."

"I can be at times," I quickly replied.

"Do you remember the Sade song Smooth Operator? I always used to think she said mmm-bop-erator.

We both laughed.

"Come on! That might be a different song all together." I continued, "Let's take a moment to appreciate Sade and her timeless beauty. Man, I dig her."

"Hah. Buttercup the sugar baby. Must be your last name!"

The landowner of the valley walked over, smiling. I had been driving with an Obama 08' bumper sticker and was now being asked to park my car out of sight. Worrying about a bumper to shotgun collision, I gracefully complied. I wasn't extremely political, but my liberal slant had made my situation a little worse. He wasn't threatened by me in the least and I hoped my defiance in not removing it showed that I felt similar.

"I see you hid your car. That free advertising is going to cost you detail work," he said, laughing.

"More than that, probably, if I am going to need a new bumper," I muttered.

"You better watch it, or I will go get my twelve gauge."

Everyone laughed.

By now a small group had gathered, all of them chuckling. The landowner joined them, talking to the foreman of each crew. He was an older man, sturdy, balding with a white goatee and aviator sunglasses. My father was close to him and shared similar political views. It seemed wherever I went lately I was the odd man out. I felt insecure as I listened to their discussion, staring out across a nearby field at a giant cross-shaped window in a barn, a homage to the savior I had left behind.

After work I decided to take a detour to Buena Vista Park in Alma, Wisconsin, one of the most beautiful overlooks in the Mississippi River Valley. Driving up the hill road which wound sharply around the bluff, I reached the empty parking lot at the top, got out of the car and stretched my legs. I ambled past rusted swing-sets to the edge of the cliff. *What would it be like if I jumped to my death right now? What would my family think? Where would I go?* I thought to myself. I imagined screaming as I dove headfirst into a rocky outcropping near the bottom of the bluff. Would I regret it halfway down? I knew it wasn't normal to think these thoughts but the way my life had gone more recently I wondered why they didn't pass through my mind more often. Of course, I didn't want to die. I just wanted my situation to improve. What would have to take place for that to occur? I wasn't sure.

I tried to imagine what the vista once looked like, mentally subtracting the buildings and roads. Not far from here two massive smokestacks towered. A couple were making their way to the cliff. I greeted them in passing and tried to practice the compassion Buddhists spoke so much about. Pausing for a moment by the playground equipment, I looked up at the darkening sky, feeling insignificant.

23

I had located a Buddhist community near Red Wing while searching online. They functioned under a European Lama and the Karmapa, a Lama similar to the Dalai Lama. I didn't know what a Karmapa was, so I pulled up my internet browser and began reading about him. The previous Karmapa had died in 1981 and was meant to reincarnate, his most loyal monks being left in charge of finding his successor.

On a Wednesday evening I made the drive down the river going south to meet the organization comprised of lay Buddhists like myself. These individuals were far less exotic than the Cambodians. They were westerners practicing the ancient art of meditation in English. It was something I desperately wanted to experience.

I pulled up to a house in the tiny city of Maiden Rock, Wisconsin. Strolling up the front walk I paused, gathering my courage a little before knocking on the heavy wooden door. An intelligent looking Asian man with short black hair and glasses answered.

"Hi! Welcome. My name is Vincent. We were just about to get started. If you'd like to come in we are having some tea in the kitchen."

He led me through a meditation room piled with stacks of cushions as well as an altar with beautiful Buddha statues. They were unfamiliar as I always thought the buddha was fat and happy. A thin cross-legged Buddha with a serene face seemed wrong to me. In the kitchen there was a large table surrounded by heavy cedar chairs. A Latina woman sat in one, stirring her tea. She was incredibly small with short, dark, curly hair and massive gold hoop earrings. Her name was Maria and I was enthralled.

"So, I have some big news, guys," she exclaimed, her accent thick. "I am moving back to Mexico City to earn a doctorate, studying cancer."

"That's great!" said Vincent enthusiastically. "But doesn't that mean we won't see you anymore?"

"Yes, sorry. I have a chance to further my education and I need to take it. Besides I wasn't really doing much here. This town is so tiny, and I miss Mexico."

This was a smaller group than the Cambodians and I could tell her departure was somewhat of a blow, though here I was, as if by magic, to replace her. I thought it was a strange coincidence that she was from Mexico, thinking of my film. *A lot of people are from Mexico,* I reminded myself ,after beginning to ruminate on my dreams a little. Perhaps she would be killed if the cartels thought she knew someone like me. I shook my head and dismissed the thought.

It was a shame she'd be leaving. It was the first time I'd fancied a woman since the fantasies about Mei had taken hold. I sat down, sorting through the tea selection.

"It's time for the talk to begin, so please grab a cushion and have a seat," Vincent instructed.

The talk was similar to a sermon in a Catholic church, but this time I was actually interested in what was being said. During the meditation that followed I dreamt that Buddha was bathing me in comfort. After the practice ended, I smiled, feeling blissful and mellow. I especially liked the line that promised, "All beings are Buddhas, whether they know it or not." It was a new take on the Christian precept, "Treat others as you wish to be treated." Being a Buddha sounded fine to me.

Next was a discussion of upcoming events. There would be a retreat the following weekend at a center an hour or so away. Vincent needed a ride and I agreed to pick him up. I didn't realize that he was a Doctor of Theology and a high-level Buddhist, having spent several years in the seminary. I was intrigued by this man affectionately dubbed "the Buddha-father."

I picked Vincent up that Saturday. An older gentleman with years of experience, he was wise but at one point unexpectedly silly, ironically making the sign of the cross on himself. Apparently, Vincent thought being blessed in two separate religious contexts couldn't hurt anything. I experienced a spike of frustration; I wished I had his eclecticism and sense of ease. My own once-strong faith in the Church had turned sour.

We drove on through the farmland, passing Amish travelers in a horse and buggy. Thoughts drifted like passing clouds and I made no attempt to determine the shapes they formed -- forever changing, morphing into opposing points of view.

"What was it like in the seminary, Vincent?"

"Well, you know, Jesus this and Bible that. Six years is a long time to study one man."

"I almost joined a seminary once, though I am glad now that I didn't because I love women so much," I confided. "By the time they sent me literature I had already lost interest."

"I'm glad you didn't because then you might not be here with me now. Why did you decide to join in the first place?" he asked.

"Well, a family friend was very Catholic, and he was persuading me to become a priest. Needless to say, he was indoctrinating me. This one time I stayed at his cabin with him. It was just him and I a few hundred yards into the woods from the main house where my father was staying. He tried to crawl in bed with me and told me he wanted to snuggle."

"Wow. No wonder you didn't want to become a priest anymore."

"Yeah," I frowned. "The guy was a pervert."

We drove through many rural villages on our way to the retreat land. I gazed out the window, my elbow resting on the sill and my hand supporting my head. Suddenly I had a thought.

"Vincent?"

"Yes, what is it?

"Do you think you can get post-traumatic stress disorder from things that happened in past lives?"

"Well, that is a good question. I guess I had never thought of that."

"Like, what if that is what mental illness is? We are still in distress about something that happened to us lifetimes ago."

"That's an interesting thought," Vincent returned. "I used to be obsessed with my past lives. I had all sorts of stories made up about who I was, up until about ten lives back. Eventually I realized it didn't really matter. It only mattered who I was now. You bring up an interesting point though. I will have to think on that."

I smiled and continued my watch over the budding fields. We passed tillers and turbines until we reached a long, nearly hidden driveway, then up a steep hill and into a wooded area. Vincent and I arrived as a meditation began and I sat down on the grass next to him. A woman sitting in front of me poked my leg.

"You can't sit in on this meditation if you are new," she informed me.

I looked around as though she was talking to someone else.

"Seriously?" I whispered.

"Yes," she inaudibly mouthed back.

Apparently, this was a high-level practice and I couldn't participate. Instead, I wandered inside a nearby building and was greeted by about twenty Buddhists who had come from all over the world for lessons from traveling teachers. They seemed an incredibly joyful group. We all crowded into the tiny gompa, or meditation room, for a talk and meditation. The heat from our bodies was making the space into a furnace that 'Om'ed when it was lit. The building was now alive, vibrating with compassion. I got a feeling like I was hearing cathedral bells in December but quickly dismissed it, disgusted. *This was completely different*, I told myself.

After the meditation I met Vincent in the dining area. He had decided to spend the night at the retreat land and let me know that I could leave if I wanted to. He gave me a copy of a book about his Lama's journey into Buddhism and smiled a mischievous grin. I gratefully accepted and smiled back, saying goodbye to my new friends and looking forward to joining their cause.

Daniel

24

On a hot summer afternoon Levi and I are eating lunch outside a crowded cafe. It is a Mexican restaurant. Levi is having enchiladas and I am sipping on a Juaritos soda. I look out over the dirty street. When was it last cleaned? I stare down at my empty plate. I always eat so fast.

"You know, I've been thinking that all my trouble with women stems back to certain instances when I have mistreated them in the past. It's almost like women I meet can sense that I did that. I feel like I used people," I confided.

"I don't think you really mistreated anyone, Daniel. I was there. Yeah, you had your flings in high school, but we all did. Don't worry about it," he replies.

"What about that time my cousin and I fooled around with the same girl within weeks of each other. I feel really shitty about that. Or, that time I kissed Zachary's girlfriend when I was drunk, and they broke up."

"Don't worry. I'm sure they have all forgotten about that."

"I just feel so bad about certain things," I continue. "Everything I've done this past year or two has been to atone for it. I feel like such a bad person. My treatment of women and my drug use... I want to become a better person."

"Listen, Daniel," Levi begins, running his hand through his hair with exaggerated patience. "I'm telling you; I was there, and you weren't this big bad person. I don't know why you think that at all."

Just then, a filthy, windowless van speeds around the corner, screeching to a halt just outside the cafe. Three masked men burst out of the front, shouting. One of them heaves open the side door and a foul smell wafts through the air. They begin pulling dead bodies out of the van, piling them up on the side of the street. Heads, limbs, so much gore, the corpses heaped on the sidewalk. My gaze locks on a pair of feet near mine, on the soles of their shoes. Chairs are being scraped back; people are gagging. Chaos erupts in the cafe as the van speeds away. Families are screaming, running away in the opposite direction. I turn to Levi.

"That's what happens to people from my past who threaten my reputation," I smile like a demon.

I lifted myself up and sat on the edge of the bed. It was a deeply troubling dream. I was uneasy. I thought this had all ended after my visit to the hospital. Why was I still feeling so guilty? Maybe nightmare Levi was right, and I shouldn't be so hard on myself. I was just like any teenager making mistakes. Wasn't I? The dream really made me question my motivations. I didn't want to hide what I did, certainly not going as far as dumping bodies on the street. What was wrong with me that I would have a nightmare like that? Why was I comparing myself to a cartel thug? I didn't intend anything bad for anyone.

I went to the bathroom to get a drink of water and pee. When I was done, I lay in bed for a long while, staring at the ceiling and trying to understand what it all meant. I thought of Maria, the Buddhist girl who had gone to Mexico City. I associated traumatic things happening with Mexico, where traumatic things *did* happen with regularity. Were these things happening to her? I rolled over and tried to get some sleep.

The next day I went to work in the scalding sun. My skin was darkening to bronze. I was averaging two or three pallets a day which sometimes meant as much as a ton of stone to be processed. I wiped my forehead with a wet and muddy glove, longing for the ice-cold spring water. It was still cool in the morning but by mid-afternoon the lukewarm spray filled with stone dust made cutting all the more miserable. I took my earplugs out and yelled to Zeke.

"Hey! Come help me with this."

I pointed down at a large piece of flat rock.

"What's the matter, Buttercup? Can't lift a little rock alone?"

I staggered back, becoming lightheaded and dropping down to one knee. I glared up at Zeke with a weary face.

"What's your story, man?" I called out.

He laughed and smiled his snaggle-tooth grin.

"If I throw my back out you will be lifting them all yourself," I continued.

After my stay last year in the Mayo Clinic psych ward I had been prescribed new medication for bipolar disorder. My current psychiatrist, Doctor Holland, had changed the prescription and now when it became hot and sunny, I felt nauseous and dizzy. I wasn't sure if this was due to side-effects or just a coincidence, so I made an appointment to see him in the Twin Cities.

"Zeke!" I tried to get his attention by tapping him on the shoulder. He took out his earplugs and I continued, "I have to leave early today. I have a doctor's appointment."

"A doctor? You wimp," he retorted.

"Whatever, Morning Glory."

I left the job site two or three hours earlier than usual to make the drive to Minneapolis. I put the car on cruise and messed with the compact disc player. To me psychiatry was a manipulative science. In theory, you tell the doctor how you feel, and he helps you get to a destination you both agree on. Doctor Holland seemed to believe choosing was his responsibility and I didn't want anyone else having that much control over my life. He was the cold, calculating type and he saw the world in black and white. I felt like psychotherapy was more constricting than liberating, though I had heard of some practitioners applying mindfulness to their techniques. A positive development maybe, but then again, Buddhism was not a cure for mental illness.

I pulled into the clinic, walked through the double glass doors and into the waiting line. These offices were always so dreary. I checked in and found a place among the blank faces waiting to see mental health professionals. As I sat there it occurred to me that the illnesses they treated were more like neural deficiencies or dysfunction within a family. More to do with chemicals and environment — parents and siblings — than the actual experience of consciousness. I imagined leaving my family to become a monk, destroying any type of hindrance they might be causing me. What could I do about the medication, though? I felt as though I had been burned, frustrated. I didn't want to take it. I dismissed the thought, remembering what happened the previous fall and quickly deciding that I needed the medicine.

The doctor eventually called my name and welcomed me into his office. The man was stale, an archaic fossil who had probably been practicing since the 1970s.

"So, how are we today?" he asked.

"Not good, doctor. I have been getting sick at work," I frowned. "I spend all day cutting stone in the sun and it is making me weak and nauseous."

"That is a side effect of the lithium. It sometimes becomes a toxin and dehydrates in direct sunlight," the doctor informed me.

"Well, I work outside on ninety-degree days. What would you recommend I do?" I replied, exasperated.

"Just wear a hat and long sleeves. Also, drink plenty of water."

"Long sleeves in this weather?!"

I was frantic.

"You'll be fine," he said, attempting to calm me.

What was I letting him do to me? I knew the weather could kill someone by itself and now he was giving me poison to finish the job? This new medication was cheaper than the original script and was all I could afford. I didn't have an argument about that so I knew the sickness would continue. It was absurd but I would have to endure it.

"Don't worry. You'll be fine."

"Fine?" I stressed. "I better be more than fine."

"You'll be fine," he repeated, deadpan.

This was clearly a question of ethics. Which was the more important, my health or my bank account? On a more expensive medicine I might not have the money to drive to the Buddhist center every week. The entire psychiatric profession was quackish. Bipolar Disorder was just another description for having feelings. Wasn't it? I couldn't really argue at this point though, so I took the slip of paper and left him to carry on poisoning others.

I had missed work several days because of my illness and I suppose the money I lost could have paid for the better medication. You couldn't really plan for things like that, though. I was about ready to say, "Fuck this guy" and be done with it. The cost of my antipsychotic was astronomical, and the lithium didn't seem to be beneficial. When you settle for a less expensive drug you get what you pay for. The more I thought about it the angrier I became. I shot daggers at the doctor as I left his office.

After the appointment I drove slowly back to Red Wing. I decided to stop at my father's house to explain what was happening to me. He met me at the door with his tiny excuse for a dog. He was concerned about my absenteeism. When the little Yorkie jumped at my legs, I picked him up, putting him down on the bench near the door.

"What did the doctor say?" my father inquired.

"Apparently he is the one who has been poisoning me."

"Don't say that. You know he is just trying to help," he replied firmly. "Your health is important to me. You know that, Daniel."

"I know that. I just wish there was something more I could do about it. The lithium is a toxin in sunlight," I conceded.

"I see. Did he give you something else?

"Fuck no. He might as well have just said, 'Daniel, it's time for you to put on your big boy pants.'"

My Dad frowned.

"We don't talk much these days, but your mother called me wondering how you were doing. She said you haven't called her in a while. Why is that?" he asked.

"I don't know. I just don't want to bother her with my personal problems."

"Just give her a call when you get a chance," he encouraged.

"Alright, Dad. I will."

I felt helpless, like an innocent man doomed to serve a life sentence, and for what? For having dreams about murdered Mexicans? For loving the wrong woman? For deviating from my Christian faith? I had made my choices and now I had to live with them. However frustrating it was, if it kept me out of trouble, I had to accept it. This mental illness could not be tolerated without medication and guidance, or so I was told. *At least I'm not in actual prison*, I mused. *At least I've gotten through my teenage years unscathed. At least I am alive. Keep your head down, Daniel*, I thought to myself. *Just keep your head down.*

25

Anna's father had commissioned me to paint a portrait that he could give his wife for her birthday. Using an old photo of her, it was my job to capture the beauty of his love.

Ahmed was a large Persian bodybuilder and when he asked you to do something, you did it. He had renounced Islam after moving to the United States and now spent most of his time watching twenty-four-hour news channels. I agreed to paint the portrait because Ahmed scared me a little. When it was finally finished, I drove to the other side of Red Wing to present it to his wife. She was ecstatic and Ahmed was pleased with my work. He offered to take me out to dinner in Saint Paul as a reward.

A few weeks later I picked up Ahmed for dinner at a Middle Eastern restaurant called The Fertile Crescent. It was a warm, late summer evening and the sun was just beginning to sink low in the sky. He barked out directions as I drove up Highway 61 into Saint Paul. He was a regular and the owner of the restaurant came out from the kitchen as soon as we arrived. He wanted to greet Ahmed personally. Ahmed told him that I was a special guest because I had done him a favor. He ordered the buffet for both of us and we sat down in a room that looked more like a cafeteria than a restaurant. He made me nervous, but I figured that if I was a friend of Anna's he was harmless enough. Scooping mouthfuls of couscous, he started the conversation.

"Do you think Levi will misbehave again?"

I felt blindsided. What was he talking about?

"Will he do what?" I asked, confused.

"Do you think Levi will start using drugs again?"

Suddenly I realized there was a little hook in this bait. He wanted information.

"What makes you think that he would ever even think of doing that? He is a family man now," I reminded him.

"My daughter still talks to me about her personal life," he replied. "Your friend has been worrying her with his previous tendencies. She says he might be thinking about selling drugs to make extra money."

I corrected him.

"You mean her husband? I don't know what you're talking about. Levi would never do that."

"Yes, my daughter's husband…" He trailed off.

Just then a group of men with slicked back hair and gold jewelry walked by our table. He turned to them to see who was walking by and back around, looking directly at me and raising both eyebrows.

"I wouldn't want anything to happen to the two of you," he threatened.

The men stopped at our table. One put his hands on the surface, got right in my face and conveyed a smile that looked more like a grimace than a grin.

"Yeah. We wouldn't want anything to happen to you," he hissed and slapped my face gently with a dirty hand.

I was staring down at my food. The men had passed without incident and Ahmed sat glaring at me from across the table.

"Hello, Daniel, come back to reality," he snapped his fingers a few times.

I placed my thumb and index finger on the bridge of my nose, lowering my head and squeezing my eyes closed.

I felt it might have been a message of intimidation to Levi and I, as though Ahmed had asked them to walk by at that particular moment. Why was I hallucinating? It was clear that I was afraid but what good would scaring me do? Since he knew everyone I wondered if that scene had been planned. I brushed the thought off as paranoid. I released the bridge of my nose and looked up at Ahmed.

"Ah, I see you are back now," he chuckled. It seemed sadistic. He continued, "You are Levi's friend and know him well. You have a history with him, and I need to know if he is trustworthy. I know all about you two. There is no reason to hide it."

The previous exchange hadn't sat well with me and I tried not to look uncomfortable.

"Dependable, yes," I replied. "I think he is a good father. Back then it was just a lapse in judgement. I don't see how it would be possible for him to sell anything. He was never like that back then. I think it takes a certain type of person."

"You two used to get in trouble together in high school. That was a long time ago and you grew apart. Maybe there are things you don't know."

"Back in high school, yeah. You're right. I don't know what happened after that."

"And in college?"

Levi was a 4.0 student. I was not close with him when he was in college and could only assume he continued drinking and possibly smoking pot every now and then. Wasn't that normal for a college kid? I began to wonder if Anna knew something that I didn't, and if she had purposely or absent-mindedly mentioned something to her father.

"I don't know. I didn't go to college with him. In high school he was the quiet one. I was the friend pushing the limits. He was always a good

143

student and got straight A's. I think he got straight A's in college too. As you know I changed, hopefully you see that he did not."

He seemed pleased with that answer, leaning back in his chair. The onslaught was over, and I breathed easier as the tension dissipated.

"Are you happy with him as a son-in-law?" I asked.

It felt awkward talking about this in public; I was covering for Levi when I wasn't sure what was going on myself.

"No, I am upset with him. He's cheap and sometimes he seems like a degenerate. If Anna hadn't loved him since you three were small, I would try to get rid of him."

"Well, I hope that changes."

"For his sake," he added.

Poor Anna. I couldn't imagine what it must have been like living with Ahmed. I could only think of how fiercely protective of her he must have been. If it were me, I would feel claustrophobic. Levi once told me that he was a man who knew how to play the system. I definitely didn't want to be on the receiving end of that expertise. I would have to pick my battles. Challenging him now did not seem like it was in my best interest.

When we were done eating, I followed behind Ahmed to the exit of the restaurant. Before we got to the door, he turned and waved goodbye to the owner. He glanced over at me.

"Did you get enough to eat then?" he asked.

"It was delicious," I said, nervously smiling.

I am pretty sure he thought I was stupid, though I didn't mind. Finding out what would happen if he felt threatened by me was something I never wanted to know. I let the subtle warning roll off my back. I was beginning to suspect that Levi had a darker history than I previously imagined. Til now I'd never given any thought to his time in college; the studious teenager he had been was slowly vanishing from my mind. Who was Levi deep down? Maybe he had been a big drug dealer in college, selling meth to make a buck and using it to study all night. Maybe that was how he got his good grades. Perhaps Ahmed was a part of the Persian mafia and there was about to be a turf war. Was I being naive? Was Ahmed just paranoid? The painting was like a peace offering met with weapons grade uranium.

After an intense silence on the way home, I dropped him in the near empty lot outside of his apartment building.

"Thanks for dinner," I yelled out after him as he exited the vehicle. He turned and stuck his head back into the car.

"I hope you are trustworthy, Daniel. I think you are a good man. Don't disappoint me."

I choked down a hard swallow and tried to smile.

I forced out a strained, "I won't."

"Good. Thank you for the painting. See you next time."

I almost hoped there wouldn't be a next time.

"Take care," I waved as he shut the door.

I watched him make his way past the security door and into the building. When he was finally gone, I breathed a sigh of relief. I felt as though I had dodged a bullet this time. The fact that I was getting shot at in the first place worried me. Something was seriously wrong here, but what? I pulled out of the parking lot and turned onto the empty street that would lead me back to my place. What was Levi getting himself into?

26

When your work is seasonal you never really know what to expect after the fall. The ground had begun to freeze, and I was only working one or two days a week. My father had let most of the other workers go for the winter. With this newfound time alone I began preparing my movie, planning to enter it in a few film festivals. It had been almost a year since I had attempted to settle my karmic debt with it. I still wanted people to see it but was afraid of how the criminal element would respond to its message.

I saw myself being targeted, threatened, beaten up, or worse, ending up in a body bag like the victims in my dreams. In one scenario three men dragged me off the street and into an empty garage, smacked me around a while then maneuvered me into an office chair, tying my hands behind my back with cable ties. "So, you want to be the next Nancy Reagan, eh, gringo?" says the tall one. "Just say yes." I tried to kick out, then to edge the chair away from them but once they realized that the chair had wheels, they pushed me from man to man, punching me full in the face. Next they wrestled off my boots. One of the guys was over in the corner. There was the sound of clanking metal. He must have been rummaging in a tool kit. He pulls out a pair of pliers and holds it up. I screamed as he approached, and I didn't recognize my own voice, it was so desperate. A dirty rag was stuffed in my mouth.

My own fear had once again become a stumbling block. I didn't really need exposure, I couldn't risk it, even assuming the film was widely distributed and well received. The main thing was to get its message out. But how? If I put it down, I could always come back to it, right? Perhaps when I had a little more mental clarity and my mind was in a healthier place.

In the meantime, I was set on meeting the Lama and learning more about his thoughts on the world. Vincent had offered to accompany me to a retreat on the east coast. It would be expensive. Money was something I didn't have but I desperately wanted to meet this holy man. The date was set and soon I would make the thousand-mile journey to a resort just outside New York City.

Two weeks later I headed to Maiden Rock to pick up Vincent. We would follow Interstate 90 through Chicago, until it turned to Interstate 80, all the way to New York state. It really reminded me of when I had tried to visit Mei in Baltimore, only this time I would actually go and meet my destiny. Perhaps this was the trip I had been meant to make. I programmed the destination into my GPS. It would take us roughly twenty-four hours to reach the resort.

It felt good to be on the open road. Driving into Madison we stopped at a Park and Ride. It seemed I was always headed east but every route I took was to a dead end. Levi's publishing company had disbanded some time ago and now he was focusing on taking care of his kids. Was Detroit now a specter from my past? I could see Levi here at this service station preparing for our trip. My mind was playing tricks on me. As we pulled back out onto the highway, I was grateful to take my mind elsewhere. Vincent began expounding his state of the union.

"It's a vicious cycle," Vincent said, removing his glasses, blowing on them and wiping them on his shirt. "The economy rises and falls over and over like history repeating. It will never stop."

I played the skeptic.

"Do you think it repeats itself because we think it will? Maybe we'll end up climbing forever if we don't sabotage ourselves with mindless repetition."

"No, it has been proven throughout history that it will repeat."

He missed my point a little, but I didn't want to call him on it.

"Yeah, the march of war, peace and revolution continues," I smirked.

"Going against it is pretty much suicide," he admitted.

There was a short silence.

"What happens when a Buddhist commits suicide?" I asked.

"Well, my understanding is that they will be reborn into a similar situation. They will be forced to solve the problem and learn the lesson. If they continue to engage in that sort of behavior it will just keep repeating in an endless loop."

"I see," I replied. "Seems like that would motivate people to keep on living. Maybe this world is the endless loop we need to get out of."

"Yes, I would say so. You hit the nail on the head!" he agreed.

After several hours Vincent took the wheel and I became navigator in the passenger seat. It was a title alone since we had the GPS. I mostly just fiddled with the radio dial when we got out of range of the previous station. Half-asleep I looked over at him. He reminded me of a bare-faced saint.

We arrived in New York the following morning. We walked in through a golden set of revolving doors and registered at the front desk. Besides being driving partners Vincent and I would also be roommates for the three-day course. We had made it in one piece and as I drifted off to sleep for the afternoon, I felt excited for the coming days.

I awoke a few hours later. Vincent had been downstairs and let me know that the Lama had arrived. I changed my clothes, wandered down to the conference hall, and found a chair next to Maria, who had come all the way from Mexico City. After twenty minutes or so a short, balding man in a purple polo shirt and camouflage pants walked in. He gave an hour-long talk on meditation, and afterward the new students were told to get in line to take refuge. Having never met the Lama, Maria and I got in line.

"How is the fight against cancer?" I asked her.

"It rages on, but I am learning a lot. How is everything in Wisconsin?"

"The same as always. I've gone to a few courses at the retreat center since you left. We've missed you. What is the Mexico City group like?"

"We are one big happy family."

I put my hands in my pockets and looked down sheepishly.

"So, any guys in Mexico City?" I asked.

"Yeah, there are plenty," she replied, laughing. "But none with me. What about you?"

"Ahhh…" I rolled my eyes. "No guys. No."

"Not what I meant!" she exclaimed.

I laughed.

"No girls either!" I added.

"Well, if you come down to Mexico City maybe I can hook you up with someone," she smirked.

"Might have to take you up on that one."

I let my eyes run the length of her body and she caught me looking. Panicked, I quickly diverted my attention to the Lama. I blushed and shyly looked back at her but she was now looking out across the crowded room. It was just my luck to get caught in something like that. Most guys would have been a little smoother about it.

We neared the Lama and she received refuge first. In Catholic confirmation each person receives a new name. The same tradition applies to Buddhism. I stood in front of the Lama as he blessed me and gave me my refuge name, Steady Light Rays. He held my forehead up against his and smiled. I didn't have much time with him as the line kept moving. A woman standing nearby handed me a string blessed by the

Karmapa. Soon after, Vincent approached with pictures taken to capture the memories.

"How does it feel to officially be Buddhist?" Vincent asked.

"Awesome! I like it," I beamed.

I lingered in the large meditation space by myself for a while, outside the large group that had formed around the stage. I felt euphoric. *Perhaps the Lama would recognize my greatness and ask me to join him on his trips around the world*, I thought. *Maybe I could become one of his most loyal students, bending to his every request.* My mind ruminated on this a bit before I dismissed the thought. Was I allowing mania to sneak back into my life? I made it upstairs to find Vincent getting ready for bed. I went into the bathroom and quietly opened my bag, removing two small orange pill bottles from a zippered compartment. How could I take them at a time like this? Did I really need these pills? I remembered the Lama and my visions of traveling with him. Reluctantly I poured a pill from each container and swallowed them. Curling up in bed I felt disenchanted as I recounted the events of the day. *You're nothing but an imperfect Buddhist*, I thought. *Your mind will never be like the Lama's.* I felt a shudder run through my body. How did this medicine fit into my new beliefs? Did they contradict each other? I lay there for a long while listening to Vincent's heavy snoring. It was an hour before I finally fell asleep. The following morning would be the first full day of meditation.

I awoke excited and hurried downstairs. The room was alive with people, vibrating with the quiet conversations of hundreds of Buddhists. It was the biggest meditation in the small group's North American history, with over five hundred and fifty people in attendance. I sat close to the stage. It was recommended that first-time students sit closer for the most positive karmic results. The Lama made his way through the crowd. Jumping up onto a highchair in front of the audience, everyone applauded as he sat in full lotus. There was to be a brief question and answer session before the meditation would begin. I listened patiently, having scribbled an inquiry on a piece of paper in my pocket. I raised my hand nervously. Eventually a woman appeared next to me with a handheld microphone.

"Yes, tell us," the Lama said, looking toward me.

"Lama, there are so many people in this world who believe it will end someday, entire institutions built around the concept."

The crowd laughed, of course thinking of the Christians.

"Your teaching on reincarnation gives me hope for the future, like we will be here for lifetimes to come," I continued. "I don't think the world will end, but wanted to ask, do you think the idea of reincarnation would help people understand the worth of the planet?"

His response was simple.

"I hope it will," he said solemnly and moved on to the next question.

This continued for another hour or so, ending in an amusing anecdote from the Lama about his hatred of American speed limits. His desire for liberating freedom also gave him a need for speed, flying down the Autobahn on a motorcycle. These things seemed like distant memories in his old age, he said, though his passions were ageless. He often took his students skydiving to make them more fearless, and almost died once after losing track of time while meditating in midair. It was no wonder that everyone was so devoted to him. His lifestyle gave the members of his community something to aspire to.

I closed my eyes and folded my arms across my chest. I could clearly see myself meditating in a meadow, as if passing the time waiting for the course to begin. Sitting on a blanket as the dander from the flowers and butterflies drifted through the air, I couldn't believe the feeling of peace that came to me. I opened my eyes, the doors closed, and the meditation began.

27

We made it to the deer park around noon on a searingly hot weekend after my high school graduation. I stepped out of the car and into the sunshine, vainly running my hand through my thick, auburn hair. My friend Eric and I had planned to eat some mushrooms and go walking in the forested area surrounding the park. Levi also came along to act as a safe person and to drive us around in his car. I had no comprehension of the precious opportunities I was squandering. Besides the drugs, with no plans for college, I spent my days much as I did now, performing backbreaking manual labor in the hot summer sun.

Eric pulled out two big plastic bags and we stared down at the dried pieces of fungus. Having all done this before we knew what we were in for, silently munching and smiling.

"Daniel, eat some of mine. I want you to trip hard," Eric said, throwing his half-eaten bag to me.

"Are you sure, man? I am not sure if I can take much more than this."

"Yeah, do it. You'll be fine," he encouraged.

Looking back, I can't say why I listened. It was already too much and I took even more. I had always been one to push it, trying to expand my mind.

We walked into the woods where the colors became more vibrant. We were talking and laughing as we went and after navigating the entire length of the trail, we rounded a corner close to the pen where the deer lived. Feeling weak I stopped and leaned on a bench close to the fence.

"I think I need to sit down for a minute, guys," I exhaled, wheezing a little.

"Are you alright?" asked Levi.

"Yeah, I will be fine. I am just tired."

I collapsed on the ground.

The world was spinning. It had been half an hour since we dosed, and the drugs were now taking full effect. I had eaten so many of them. My feelings and impressions were beyond my control, roiling waves of fear and dread. I moved through intense states of consciousness while my body lay prone and corpse-like. Entering a dream within a dream I moved through the hedges of my mind, its infinite concentric maze. Levi shook me, shook my motionless body then dragged me into the car. He drove me to several places, trying to decide what to do with the dead looking friend in the back seat. He took me to his girlfriend's place and left me in the car. Levi must have panicked after we arrived, not knowing what else to do with me. I baked inside the car in the afternoon heat. Waking, I squirmed and flailed my limbs violently in an attempt to kick out the back window, my vision still clouded like a static-filled television screen. Somehow, I managed to find the door handle and open it, crawling out onto the street. There I lay on my back gasping for air, where anyone could have come and run me over.

I am not sure who called the paramedics. I only remember their concerned faces as they strapped me to a gurney and lifted me into the back of the ambulance. Upon reaching the hospital I had my stomach pumped, lying on the table, still unable to control my body. In a moment of peace, I shifted my head to the left where a county sheriff was eyeing me suspiciously. Was I about to be arrested? I couldn't tell what was happening. They had cut off my clothes and I lay on the table stark naked. I looked straight ahead to where my father stood. My mother was at my side wiping the sweat from my forehead and telling me everything would be alright. In an effort to curb this kind of behavior and remove any excess poison from my system they produced a large catheter. Like a newborn baby, I was completely vulnerable. I knew they were going to hit me where it hurt. I squeezed my eyes shut and everything went dark as they jammed it in. My back arched. The pain was so severe I passed out. My consciousness seemed to exit through the top of my head and as it floated above my body I didn't know if I had died.

Now I was in a sun-kissed meadow, lying on a grassy knoll surrounded by jewel-like butterflies. I stretched my arms behind my head and gazed up into the deep blue sky. If this was heaven, Saint Peter was nowhere to be seen. I felt the benevolent presence of an airborne spirit. Who was she and why couldn't I see her? I can only imagine now that she was a presence who didn't want me to die. I knew then that I needed to find a love equal to that emanating from this euphoric spirit, my goal in life must be to experience this. I had to go back because I didn't yet know who this disembodied person was. Impossible to explain, but I now knew that heaven existed.

It seemed as though I stayed in the meadow a while longer and somehow, by the time it was all over, I was standing with one of the nurses on the curb outside the hospital. What had transpired and why couldn't I remember? I felt cleansed, tired and happy. I had survived the ordeal and I think the police felt sorry for me, threatening no legal action.

"You are lucky to be alive," the nurse scolded me. "Those mushrooms you ate were poisonous. That is what happens when you do drugs. You should reevaluate how you are spending your time."

"I will try," I replied meekly.

I now felt embarrassed that everyone had seen me naked, exposed. I spent the next few days staying with my father. It was strange because my family had had no reason to interfere with my drug use until now. Mushrooms weren't addictive but there was so much under the surface of my overdose. Pot was one thing that they figured into their concern. They didn't know about the prescription pain medications, methadone, oxycontin, Percocet, or the cocaine. The tip of the iceberg was finally in plain view, but what of the depths? I couldn't tell them. I would act like it was just pot and mushrooms. I didn't want to worry them more than they already were.

I wondered what had happened to Levi after that fateful afternoon. Had he also found a life free from the pressures of addiction or had he gone further down the rabbit hole? It seemed everything I had learned about him during the past few years, about his wife Anna and their children, might have been a cover story for a horrible truth. Maybe Levi was a dealer, caught up in a murky underworld. Maybe he only pretended to be my friend. He might be relaying information about my film to people who could hurt me. Or was I just paranoid and looking for answers to questions I'd never believe the answers to anyway? Whatever Levi had done, it had nothing to do with my own mental breakdown. Or did it? I couldn't say for sure. I only felt there was something going on behind the curtain. It seemed as though unseen forces were guiding our friendship down a dark path. As for Levi, I supposed that Anna might save him. *But what about me?* I wondered. There was no miraculous answer. I could only hope that my spirituality would guide me to a place of certainty.

I opened my eyes, bringing my awareness to my surroundings. Hundreds of tranquil Buddhists sat with their eyes closed in lotus position. I breathed a heavy sigh and closed my eyes again, focusing my mind on its own liberation, attempting to escape the suffering on this plane of existence.

28

Vincent and I arrived home three nights later. It had been an uneventful ride back to Maiden Rock and we were both grateful to be sleeping in our own beds. I dropped him off at his apartment and then drove across the bridge to Red Wing. In the morning I braved a small amount of traffic to make it to Dr. Holland's office in the Twin Cities. On the way I had a chance to think over what had happened last time. I felt a confrontation coming on, knowing that I had to say something more about what had taken place.

The doctor called my name from the hallway as he always did and offered me a seat in one of his expensive padded chairs. He sat down behind the desk, back straight, pulling the chair forward while maintaining a rigid posture.

"How have you been? It's been a while since your last visit."

"Honestly, Doctor, I am hoping to find a holistic way to treat my disorder," I began.

I didn't want to say anything about the Lama. After all, he didn't need to know. He looked surprised and must have thought me naive, believing that there was no effective alternative to his treatment.

"As a race, humans have existed for thousands of years without psychiatry, therapy or medications. Why now is it more important than in previous decades when we were fine without them? America survived the Great Depression without Prozac," I declared, defending my request.

"You need medication to function normally. You either take what is prescribed or face hospitalization. If I take you off medication, next thing you know you'll be in Mexico trying to write the great American novel."

"And what would be wrong with that? That sounds like an ultimatum. At least I would be following a dream. I feel like, as a society, we have set a standard for ourselves. Our idea of normalcy has become like an island only a select few can fit on. The rest of us have to take pills. My question is why? We need to redefine normal in order to move forward, not declare everyone imperfect who doesn't act a certain way."

"I am sorry you feel that way. Thousands of years ago Jesus healed schizophrenics with his bare hands..." his voice became quieter as he realized what he was saying.

I couldn't believe what I was hearing. I considered this a massive breach of professional protocol and he held his tongue for a few brief moments. Was there a conspiracy in the mental health field? Were practitioners trying to persuade their clients to be Christian? I was fuming.

"You know, maybe there is a Chinese remedy," he continued, trying to smooth things over.

I stood up and slid my chair back behind me.

"Are you angry with me?" he asked, in a tense moment.

"No, I am fine," I lied. "I need to find another psychiatrist!"

I exited the office and swiftly walked out the double glass doors into the parking lot.

Christianity had become a trigger for me because the belief inspired a massive amount of guilt and shame. I felt like I was forced to believe it. I was always drawn to eastern philosophy, but it seemed that everyone was trying to pull me in a different direction. Was it really so wrong? Eternal damnation was not something I wanted anyone to go through. It just wasn't right, even for the most severe offenders. Forever? Sadistic! I also felt as though modern medicine had failed me, or at the very least these older practitioners. This wasn't the 1960s or 1970s anymore. People know that religion doesn't fix mental illness. I drove through light rain on my way home to Red Wing. Feverishly punching buttons on my cell phone with my free hand, I tried to reach Vincent. I wanted a Buddhist doctor.

"Hello, Vincent? I have a problem. My doctor just went Jesus freak on me."

"Oh, no! Is there anything I can do to help?"

"He told me Jesus could heal schizophrenics with his hands. I am not a fucking schizophrenic! I mean this is messed up, right?" I replied frantically.

"I see. Maybe there was some sort of misunderstanding."

"I don't care!" I was practically yelling. "I need a new doctor!"

"Let me see what I can do," he replied, trying to calm me.

I could tell he didn't really know what to say, and after the conversation ended, I continued to panic. Was Holland trying to force me to switch religions? I couldn't really be sure. I hated synthetic substances and wanted out of it. My diagnosis and subsequent treatment was a sentence I was unwilling to serve. The concept of the mind's perfection is important to a Buddhist and this man was trying to tell me mine wasn't, or at best that I needed Jesus to fix it.

I made my way back home anxiously, knowing that I had lost some support. Bursting through the door to my apartment I marched to the medicine cabinet and flushed every pill down the toilet. My family would disapprove but they didn't have to know. I was now free and that was all that mattered. Hopefully Vincent would help me find a new doctor, one who would understand my circumstances.

I lit some candles and sat down on my meditation cushion. My cat came to greet me, running his body against my knee. I shooed him away and placed my hand on my heart, closing my eyes. I began saying mantras and gradually my mind calmed and drifted off into a place of peace. I lost myself in the murmuring of my own voice and forgot the dramatic events that had just occurred. I breathed deeply and paused for a moment, brushing my hand against my cheek. An unexpected sob erupted from deep within my chest. Holding back tears I rushed into the bedroom and surrounded myself with blankets. The last thing I remember was the cat jumping onto the bed. I was fast asleep within minutes.

29

My father needed a few of us for the first few days in December. It hadn't yet snowed, and we spent our time trying to hack through the frozen soil to place stones. It wasn't so bad when you bundled up. Without the sun and heat I no longer had to worry about getting sick. As though it would have mattered anyway; the poison was now out of my bloodstream.

Zeke and I were his only employees left for the winter. Today we were moving rebar to be used for construction in the spring, into the loft of the barn. I grabbed an armful of the metal rods and trudged up the stairs. I threw them, ringing, onto a large pile.

"I hate this garbage rebar. Maybe I should just skip town and get out of this place," I muttered to myself.

It was unusual that I talked to myself like this and I tried to keep my voice down. After all, I didn't want Zeke to think I was crazy. I was beginning to talk to myself more frequently since I stopped taking my medication.

"Stupid, stupid Daniel," I mouthed a bit louder as Zeke came up the stairs. I covered my mouth with my hand.

Trying to divert my attention my eyes bounced around the room. I noticed a large stone slab propped up against a wall near the stacks of rebar. Zeke dropped his pile and my heart jumped, startled by the loud noises.

"What is that?" I asked, pointing down to the slab.

"That is one of the homeowner's new onyx countertops. I think he said it was delivered here the other day from Mexico," Zeke informed.

Visions of my Mexican nightmares raced through my head. I imagined myself walking down the street at night. Suddenly a group of men emerged from a darkened ally and followed me along the pavement as the streetlights went out one by one.

"Gringo," I inadvertently whispered through my teeth, under my breath.

One of the men pulled out a switchblade knife and extended the blade with a distinct metallic click. I was running, pushing garbage bins out into the pavement behind me. Anything to stop them. My lungs were burning, and my limbs felt numb from strained muscles. My calves were on fire. I screamed.

"Gringo."

I restrained myself and my throat only produced a low guttural whisper. Shocked, I covered my mouth with my hand and Zeke gave me a funny look.

"Hey Daniel, are you still doing that Buddhist stuff?" he asked.

I muttered "Gringo" several more times. I continued covering my mouth.

"Are you alright?" Zeke asked.

"Yes, yes, I am fine," I assured him through my fingers.

"Alright. I was going to say at least you aren't a Jehovah's Witness. They came knocking on my door the other day wanting to save my soul."

"Did you invite them in?"

"I did, but I shouldn't have. They started telling me how Jesus was going to come back and be elected president of the United States," he said, laughing a little.

"Oh," I replied, trying not to say anything else under my breath. "What did you say?"

"I asked them if they were on fucking crack!"

I tried to laugh but all I could do was force a smile. My body became tense and I excused myself to an isolated corner of the barn.

"Daniel you're so stupid! Why did you waste all your money on a meditation retreat? You can't survive the winter. Stupid, stupid, stupid," I chastised myself.

Zeke called out from somewhere down below, "Who are you talking to up there, Sugar Baby?"

"No one," I replied, storming down the stairs and forcefully pushing myself past Zeke. Once outdoors I took the frigid air in deep breaths in an attempt to pull myself together.

"You can do this. Clear your mind like in the meditation," I whispered to myself, becoming perceptibly more centered, my nerves calmed, I felt more normal. I went back into the barn and we continued our work. I didn't have any more outbursts for the remainder of the day but something was clearly wrong.

Halfway through the month a white sheet of snow descended on the remote farmland and we called it a year, retiring to our couches and armchairs for the cold winter months of unemployment.

During the next few days an ache crept into my heart like the slow silent cold between the windowpanes. I sat in bed with my computer on my lap, looking for design jobs. My plan for the next month or so was to enter a self-induced Buddhist retreat in which I would meditate and study the Dharma for days on end. I sent out some emails to my Buddhist friends, asking for literature recommendations.

I stacked my meditation books in a neat little pile next to my small altar and folded a blanket on the ground for added comfort. Putting the cushion on top of that and placing my malas to the side, I sat down ready for a session, clearing my mind of all thought. I waited for a moment in complete stillness, ready to begin saying mantras, when I had an idea. My life had been such an interesting story these past few years. What would happen if I wrote it down? I ran the idea through my head as my fingers caressed the beaded necklace in my hand.

What would the Lama do? I decided that if I meditated, I wouldn't be earning anything. Being poor was a motivation and for some reason I thought the story could make money. I sat for a while longer, not wanting to give up the practice. I decided I needed to write my story, and since I had a few months, now would be the time to do it. I stood up and walked into the bedroom where my laptop still lay open on top of the wadded-up blankets. I sat down and wrote some brief notes, reading them several times through. Now, this would be an adventure.

For eight hours a day I wrote, hardly leaving the bed to eat or use the restroom. Showering at this point was out of the question and I was growing a beard. The only friend I had was my cat and a mild hallucination of Vincent telling me to eat. I thought obsessively about Mei. She was with me during this lonely time. The cutting board in the kitchen always triggered thoughts of her and I began, superstitiously, to associate it with her, refusing to cut my vegetables on it in case it hurt her. Day after day I wrote about the love I had lost but never had. As I wrote I pictured her reading my published words and a thrill ran through me. Dramatic thoughts wheeled about – I would have given the rest of my days just to see her once.

When not writing I would drive the backroads of the county seeking mental solace. I sometimes trailed off into other regions, following unfamiliar valleys along the Mississippi. Since my days driving through Saint Paul, I had found Mei again.

The thought burned now like a flame, like an all-consuming forest fire, igniting the dried-out timbers of long ago. The new growth that had appeared in these woods didn't stand a chance against the raging inferno of my memories. I had to have her. This hopeless desire was tearing my world apart. I pictured her watching my every move, witness to my every thought – approving, disapproving, laughing, frowning. Since I loved her, she must love me back. Love was not a one-way street.

I tried to find gas stations I hadn't yet been to, at times driving through the night because I couldn't sleep. Several times I spun my wheels on the icy highways, turning in circles and finding myself in the ditch next to barren corn fields. I always managed to find a way out and continue, inscribing the story in my thoughts to be put down in prose upon my return.

Mei had been a forbidden lure for me since the time before my hospitalization, when her pursuit had been my only need and desire. I looked back on what had happened since; traveling to Detroit only to give up on a dream, attempting to extricate myself from a crumbling friendship, abandoning the film. All my ventures had been unsuccessful. Maybe, just maybe, if I wrote about it some of these things would change or at the very least, I would perceive them differently. To love in the midst of my self-hatred and shame was a beautiful thing. My heart made itself felt, a real living organ not some schmaltzy symbol, pumping like a pair of bellows, beating stronger than it ever had before.

My grandmother's ring was now safely in her jewelry box. I decided to stop by her house so I could ask her if I could have it for a while. It had been mailed back after I left it at Lacroix, along with several other items I had forgotten to pack. I placed the ring in my coat pocket near my heart with the blessing string from the Karmapa. It had been a while since I had seen the small piece of finery. I needed an anchor, a talisman. It looked as it did, a little tarnished with the numbers fading away. I sat at my kitchen counter examining it, remembering the hardships I still seemed to be facing. How was it that I could work my hands to the bone for over a year and still see no progress? The answer lay within the ring. I followed its tiny grooves with my fingertip.

Setting it down for a moment I grabbed my camera, took a photo of it, of the hat I had purchased for our trip to Detroit, and the cutting board. When I was done, I placed the ring back in my pocket. The

Wolverines hat and Camel jacket had become like a uniform along with a ripped pair of mud-stained jeans. I traveled from place to place like a refugee, never arriving, never safe. The cloth tennis shoes without shoestrings that I wore were filthy, the second pair I had purchased were now developing holes.

"Are you telling me there is no work at all? There has to be something I can do. What about stained glass? Isn't that a side project right now?" I pleaded with my dad when I called him a bit later.

"Sorry, son, there isn't anything more and the ice is making it too difficult to landscape."

"Well, what am I supposed to do for money?" I demanded.

"You said you were looking for design work..."

"Yeah, and you said you would help me find some," I exclaimed defiantly.

The line fell silent.

"Just do what you can to conserve resources, okay?" he replied after a few moments.

"Fine."

The phone went dead. Frustrated, I had hung up.

It's safe to say I was a mess, with hardly any money and starving. It was painfully obvious now that the meditation course had been a bad idea. This position was all too familiar. I now spent the hours on the road or at the window watching the snow fall, rationing gas and food, not knowing if I would make it through the winter. *The bottom again*, I thought. I couldn't say that I missed it. Little did I know that I wasn't even close to the bottom. Where I was headed no one could save me. I had nightmares of homelessness, being left out on the street with no hope of support.

After completing the first part of my story I was searching for ways to sell it. Surely someone somewhere would see it as valuable. I sent a copy to my uncle, a retired Naval Commander. It was mostly a cry for help, but I thought maybe he knew someone who would be interested in it. Perhaps he would understand my misfortune and lend a compassionate ear. After a week or so he sent back a message, commenting how difficult it must have been for me to put my thoughts down. It was clear he sympathized with my plight though there wasn't a lot he could do. I responded with a blank document, subject line "Part Two Outline." My first draft had ended with my trip to the psych ward in Rochester. I knew a second story would end with the draft being written. I would write the third part with my whole body, the future as uncertain as my chances of survival. I wasn't sure what would happen next but knew that something had to. Trouble, both mental and financial, had found me. The question now was what would I do about it? The rest of the tale would tell itself somehow, I would be its channel and scribe.

Part Three

Corners Untouched by Madness

The kettle's hiss like snakes,
closer and further from wisdom.
The leaves like memories,
beneath the water tumbling.

I visited six service stations
in corners untouched by madness,
the hatred of plastic Freudian secrets
like torn glovebox prescriptions.

I crashed in an outskirt field,
where snowflakes cursed your name silently.
Clarity is a term for mendicants
knowing ugly impending truths.

Remembering now the hours spent,
driving insane without you.
I cried tonight alone,
caressing your genius.

30

I find myself in palatial surroundings, marble pillars and satin tapestries on the walls. Outside the door an armed guard patrols the long hallway, carrying an automatic rifle. I can see him on a large panel of television screens on the far wall. There are several more guards throughout the compound that are also on camera, so many that the monitors have to switch to different locations every ten seconds. I lay in bed next to Mei. We kiss deeply and she moves under me, wrapping her arms around my back. Her dark eyes shimmer in the dim light. The pleasure is intense, and I cry out. This is my inheritance. I am the wealthy son of a cartel drug lord. I haven't done anything to earn these spoils and I'm not really sure what they mean. Mei moves out from under me and throwing her leg over my waist, she raises herself up, straddling me. She looks fixedly into my eyes.

"This is what you get for wanting to lead an excessive lifestyle."

When I try to respond I look down and realize that I have been castrated.

I woke, shocked but aroused, from this trance invoked by a Buddhist meditation. The vision was disturbing for many reasons, but this seemed to be an omen. I looked down at the mala in my hand and realized where I was, sitting next to Vincent in the gompa of the retreat center. He looked over at me and smiled.

"Let's go have a drink," he said.

"You know, as long as it is non-alcoholic, sure."

In the kitchen he got two bottles of sparkling water from the fridge. After visiting the Theravada temple, I had spent time studying their texts in my grandmother's living room. I looked down at a scar on my index finger, suddenly realizing what it meant. It was a story about the Buddha, stuck in my mind as a simple lesson.

"You know, I haven't given a talk yet and I have been a member for nine months," I pointed out.

"Well, I would say it's about time you did," Vincent replied.

"I have one in mind, but I think it's a Theravada teaching."

"Sorry, Daniel, we only give Vajrayana lessons here."

I frowned, knowing that I had something good.

"How about if I give it to you right now?" I coaxed. "It is a teaching from literature I received from a Theravada group near the Twin Cities."

"I think I know the group you are talking about. Go ahead," Vincent agreed, rubbing his chin.

He sat down and made himself comfortable on a sofa, giving me his full attention. This was to be my first Buddhist teaching.

"A long time ago there was a man named Angulimala. He was the most brilliant student of a renowned teacher. The other students grew jealous and poisoned the teacher's mind, turning him against Angulimala. Wanting to teach him a lesson the teacher said, "If you want to be the best student, bring me one thousand index fingers from the right hand of unknowing travelers." Angulimala complied, stalking people in the night when they were walking through the forest."

Vincent leaned forward, now curious.

"It didn't take long for him to collect nine hundred and ninety-nine fingers which he threaded on necklaces, a truly frightful sight. The

Buddha himself was to be his one thousandth victim. As he walked down a darkened path Angulimala drew his sword and approached. The Buddha spoke of non-violence, and realizing who he was, Angulimala sheathed his weapon and decided to join him.

"Every day the reformed murderer went from house to house gathering alms and every day the families of his victims remembered who he was. He often arrived home, his head bloodied and crushed. His meditations were haunted by the pathetic cries of the people he had killed."

Vincent leaned back again. I raised my right hand, proudly displaying the scar on my index finger.

"This scar is a constant reminder of Angulimala's lesson. If we do evil, we will have evil done to us. It is a basic rule of karma."

Vincent looked down at his hands for a moment, then raised the same finger on his right hand. He too had a scar further down towards the knuckle. It looked jagged and painful.

"Wow, that is cool!" I laughed.

"You know, Daniel, I guess I never thought of it," he admitted.

"Have you heard that story before? I mean, how did you get yours?"

"No, I haven't actually," he conceded. "I was washing wine glasses and one broke. What about you?"

"I was spearing a hot dog and got burned on the metal poker."

We both laughed.

"Yours is a lot cooler," I had to admit.

My scar looked self-inflicted. I wanted to teach this lesson to everyone but then I supposed that even if they didn't know the story its precept must be common knowledge.

It was a Friday night before a retreat and others were scheduled to arrive soon. Vincent had shown me the ropes in a preliminary meditation and soon I would be practicing with the others. I excused myself from the dining room and wandered into the gompa to admire the artwork and statuary there.

I looked closely at the statue of the Buddha. Maybe my vision about the drug cartel was a bit like the story of Siddhartha finding there was more to life and leaving the castle for good. It was rare to see someone so privileged willingly accept a life of poverty. I felt like I could have been rich if I had played my cards right, though I wondered if I really would have been happy. It's not that I was happy now, but it made me think. I cautiously reached out and touched the statue.

I left the gompa, carefully closing the door and turning down the lights. Determined to pull my life back together I rejoined Vincent in the other room. The night was filled with laughter, but the threat of homelessness awaited me at the end of the weekend. At this point sending wishes to the Buddha wasn't quite enough.

31

During the time it took me to drive from the retreat center to my apartment my thoughts turned inevitably to Mei. If I couldn't win her, maybe I could somehow gain her favor. Then she would have no choice but to fall in love with me. I pictured myself receiving the Booker Prize for my brilliant, perfectly honed and hard-hitting novel, which had been popularly credited with opening up a new, more frank discussion about the subjects of mental health and drugs. Mei was watching on TV as I made my acceptance speech, in which I named her as sole inspiration.

I had stopped taking my medication. The more I thought about her the larger the delusions became. I knew that I would end up with her, it just had to be. I guess I knew the thought, if shared, would be branded grandiose, but it defined my reality with the bullet-proof cloak of truth.

As the financial pressure mounted the quality of my life declined. I felt suicidal. How would I do it? Pills probably. It would be kinder that way. Sometimes I lay in bed with the covers pulled up to my chin, gazing into the closet and wondering how to tie a noose. To get rid of these feelings I told myself jokes. My neighbors often heard maniacal laughter through the flimsy walls and a few times I heard them bang on their side in order to get me to stop.

I would often make jokes up when I was driving and write them down once I got home. I started a fake company called DaniLeaks and boasted that I was leaking documents back to the government. So many had been lost due to hacking that we needed to refill the vaults. Luckily my uncle, the Commander, had a sense of humor. As I sent him leak after leak, I remembered my time spent at Lacroix as a form of corporate terror. I would also send the leaks to random friends and relatives thinking that, maybe, if they were funny enough, Mei would receive one eventually. She would get my offbeat sense of humor and realize what she was missing. The plan was perfect, or so I thought. What could possibly go wrong?

Not all of the messages were meant to be funny. I drafted several about the Communist agenda to the former Navy Commander now turned government consultant. I explained that the theory was a naturally occurring thought. Trying to rid the world of Communists was like Hitler trying to dispel the Jews. We needed a permanent place for people to go who enjoyed this type of thinking and as the world turned, each country got more diverse. Give it enough time and even China would be home to people from all nations and ethnic groups. I also sent him a bundle of religious themed reports explaining how Buddhists and Christians could work together. The Commander remained silent, quietly collecting my thoughts and, for all I knew, building a case.

The documents were piling up and as I continued to write I got ideas about sending them to other sources. Gathering up the messages on religion and government, I sent several to the offices of Buddhist figureheads and to the Vatican. There was a hope that seeing things my way would inspire them to work together more. I kind of realized I was getting even more delusional but figured if there was even a minute chance it could make things more peaceful, I might as well try it. No one responded so I supposed that all of the messages were immediately deleted. The day after sending them I awoke to a curious headline: The Pope had resigned.

"Oh, shit!"

Shocked, I had no idea if those in the Vatican had read what I had written. I tried to tell myself it wasn't because of me. Of course, it wasn't, but the coincidence was confusing. Had any of the other organizations noticed this? Apparently, they had dismissed me as insane, and at that point I basically was. I calmly collected myself and decided to write a series of Jesus jokes for the retiring clergyman. Referencing both Buddhism and Christianity, I sent a batch to both the Vatican and the local diocese. Upon reading the jokes the Diocese of Red Wing finally responded.

"We are sorry to hear that you are no longer Catholic. Hopefully one day you will see the true light of God and repent your ways."

I quickly responded, tired of being chastised.

"I wrote Jesus jokes for the Pope. What did you do for his retirement?"

Even though I had sent over one hundred messages, the only people to respond were from the local Catholic Church. In all honesty though it had just been a polite way of saying, "You're going to hell." What else could possibly happen to someone in my position? My father was wondering the same thing after receiving an email about Communism. He called me on the phone.

"Son, what are you doing? You seem awfully unstable. Are you taking your medication?"

"I don't have anything better to do, besides this is fun. Of course, I am taking my medication," I lied.

"You need to go to the hospital. Do you need a ride there?"

"No, I'll be fine. I promise to stop."

"Okay, Daniel. Be safe," was his only response.

The excitement of being a terrorist was winding down. I sent my manuscript off to publishing companies. One requested that a third-party hand them the document and I noticed that they had just laid off a large percentage of their workers. I immediately responded that with the money they paid the middleman they could hire all of them back. Needless to say, they didn't read my book. Another company agreed to print it but needed seventeen thousand dollars in capital for publishing costs. I wondered if they had even read it.

I had spent the past week or so laughing in my bed. Several important religious and government entities were now aware that I really was a crazy person. I hadn't bothered with food during this time and was near starvation. My only human contact had been with gas station attendants. My bank account only had a few hundred dollars in it and rent was almost due.

I was utterly exhausted. The phone rang. I hauled myself out of bed. The name on the display read, "Levi." I felt like he was keeping tabs on me and decided to ignore him. It was mid-morning and I had been awake all night. I needed to sleep. A conversation was beyond my capabilities.

I stood for a long moment in front of the picture window in my bedroom, arms folded across my chest. There was a cafe across the street, and I watched as people came and went. They were completely oblivious to the man losing his mind across the street. I imagined Mei going on a day trip to Washington DC. Perhaps as she passed a similar cafe the Commander had bumped into her going the opposite direction. Perhaps they knew each other. As I looked out through the window, I imagined what they might say to each other now. I assumed maybe he would tell some clever joke about tensions in the South China Sea. It was true there was a standoff there between the US Navy and the Chinese Navy. Our circumstances seemed to be a bit like Romeo and Juliet in comparison. Would we also end in tragedy? The Commander was kind and told the most innocent jokes. I am sure she would have liked that about him.

Daniel

I glanced down at my phone. I felt restless. I had to get out of the apartment. Instead of getting the sleep I so desperately needed, I grabbed my jacket and headed for the door. It was time to go for a drive.

32

I walked briskly out the apartment building door and into the parking lot. I was off again to drive haphazardly through the countryside, but for the first time I was met with resistance. My father, concerned with my wellbeing, had come to meet me for a sort of intervention. He knew about the incident with Doctor Holland, assuming that I had stopped taking my medication as well. He was right but I still tried to hide that from him.

"I'm worried about you, Daniel. What's going on with you?"

He sat on my worn purple couch with a concerned look on his face.

"Nothing is going on. I am just completely broke," I replied quietly.

"What have you been doing without any money?"

"Well, I wrote a book and now I am trying to get it published," I attempted to assure him.

"Don't you think that is sort of a grandiose dream? You should be looking for a job."

The idea of another office job appalled me. I would rather be lifting rocks and digging holes. Maybe the book was a pipe dream but at least I had enjoyed writing it. I didn't know what else to say except that I would wait for spring in order to find work. There wasn't anything I would rather be doing and maybe I could find freelance design jobs until then. I had been on two job interviews earlier in the fall. Overqualified, I had been turned away. I had a lot of design experience and they were looking for entry level workers. I felt foolish being passed over but there wasn't anything I could do.

"Have you talked to Levi lately?" he asked.

"I am not going to talk to him anymore."

"But he was such a good friend to you," he pressed.

"I am concerned he is going down the wrong path. He was talking to me about addiction one day and I assume he wanted to start using drugs again," I frowned.

"Don't you think you're going down a bad path too now, son?"

I didn't think so, but my father knew I was. He had a good sense of these things and I was floundering. I remembered Ahmed's warning and suddenly it all made sense. To cover up Levi's indiscretions and to protect Anna and his grandchildren, Ahmed would place the blame on me and target me as the problem with his son-in-law.

"It has something to do with Ahmed," I admitted quietly.

"The one you painted the picture for?"

"Yeah," I confirmed.

"I thought you liked him," he replied solemnly.

In his mind Levi and Ahmed had been good for me, not making things worse. This was an unwelcome turn of events and expecting them to get me out of it now was an impossibility. My ideas about Levi and Anna's father had put unnecessary stress on the friendships. My father knew I was spiraling out of control but was powerless to assist me if I wouldn't accept his help.

"Are you sure you're going to be alright? I want you to get help," my father pleaded.

"Yeah, I should be fine until spring. I might need help with money but that's about it."

"I might be able to help you a little. Don't count on it though. I am hurting too. Your mother is planning to come down from Duluth to visit you sometime soon. Try to clean yourself up. She is worried about you."

"I understand…" I muttered under my breath.

"Your sister called me. Her new boyfriend is a therapist and she thought it might help you to talk to him. She wants you two to meet someday and maybe you can talk about what's bothering you," he offered.

"Sorry I don't think I can trust someone new right now. Especially not Jordan's boyfriend. I just need some time alone."

"You need to be with your family Daniel. We want to help you. Your mom and sister want to help you."

"I know. Just let me get through this. I don't need help right now."

He looked concerned. When he left, he gave me a hug and prayed out loud that I make it through. I tried to imagine my father's strained conversations with my uncle and mother about my strange and controversial communications. They must have been at a loss to know what to do. This conversation was the first of several that were meant to get me to a hospital.

Putting the intervention to the back of my mind, I left the apartment to go driving. The talk about Levi was bothering me. Considering that I believed the heartbreak with Mei was his and Anna's fault, I wanted revenge. Why couldn't they have taken my side? Why did they abandon me? I am not saying it wasn't retaliation but I don't believe now that it was intentional in the sense of being clearly thought out. I stayed out for much of the night, hopping from service station to service station, only coming back when I had met my allowance for gas.

I had found an old credit card and quickly began racking up charges. Gas station sandwiches, gasoline, and bottles of soda. Everything is marked up at the service station and it showed in my finances. The money wasn't mine to spend but staying at home all day was making my symptoms worse. With nothing to turn to at home, the darkened backroads were my only friends. The next day I would report Levi and Ahmed for threats and intimidation and be done with it. The final blow would be given and even the thought of Levi's children couldn't dissuade me. It was his fault I was in this mess, or so I thought.

The next day I took a parking ticket I had received for not moving my car for a snowplow along to the police station. Asking to argue it, I would hopefully be allowed entry, where I would then tell my story of threats and intimidation. I parked in the lot outside the sheriff's office and lingered by a picnic table near the squad cars. I pulled my grandmother's ring from my pocket, remembering what I had lost. A sheriff's deputy walked by and I asked him how to enter the station. He pointed me toward a side door with an intercom. Apparently, it was after hours, the ticket needing to be argued at a later date. Determined I pushed the button and waited for the metallic voice in the dispatch office to answer.

"How can I help you?"

It sounded like she was talking through a tin can.

"I have a ticket I need to argue."

"You'll have to come back tomorrow. We are closed."

"Are you sure? I really need to speak with an officer."

"Is it an emergency?"

"Yes," I replied, not wanting to tell her why I had actually come.

"Well, if you're only arguing a ticket I would say it isn't."

"I have a tip on a crime and was using the ticket as a cover." I continued, "I need to speak with an officer about it because I am feeling unsafe."

It seemed this was an odd request, but she reluctantly let me in. I was to take the elevator to a second floor waiting room where an officer would meet with me.

The elevator was a lonely minute on the way to a small room with a picture window, a few chairs and a table with a phone on it. The phone rang. I guess they wanted me to answer but knowing it wasn't my phone gave me second thoughts. I didn't pick it up. Soon after, a policeman walked in, politely asking me to answer it. When it rang again I did. Once again, I explained my reasons for being allowed into the station. The same officer then returned with another in order to get a clear picture of what was going on.

"Why are you here again?" the officer asked.

"I have a tip about some illegal intimidation, and I want protection from it."

"Where did the crime take place?"

"Saint Paul."

"Well, that is Ramsey County's problem. You will have to take it up with them."

"So, let me get this straight. I have to drive to Saint Paul?" I was getting frustrated.

"Do you want to report the crime? If it didn't happen here we can't do anything about it."

"Alright. Thanks for your time!" I yelled, already on my way down the stairwell.

I left disgruntled. It was seven in the evening and the drive to the Twin Cities would take time. I wasn't really sure why I was doing this, but all signs pointed to retribution. Earlier in my life I thought I would have been above something like this, though unusual circumstances sometimes cause people to act irrationally.

I stopped at a nearby gas station to top off my tank, pulling out my cell phone for the address of the Saint Paul Police Department. It was going to be a long night and I wanted closure. Convinced that they had put me in this hole, I would climb out again. I would not live in fear of Ahmed. After all, keeping these secrets wasn't my job. Maybe I was delusional and exaggerating the importance of events, but I was sure of two things. Levi had a dark history and Ahmed had committed a crime. I wanted him to pay for it.

I turned on my headlights and pulled out of the gas station and onto the snowy river road. I would have my justice.

33

The police station was dimly lit, and if it wasn't for the parking lot filled with squad cars, I would have missed it entirely. I walked down the icy street past a sign that read Saint Paul Police Department and toward the front of the station. After arriving inside, I passed through a tiled entryway leading to a desk encased in bulletproof glass. A woman sat behind it along with an officer reclining in a desk chair and drinking a cup of coffee. I approached several small holes in the glass in a circular pattern, leaning into speak.

"Hi there, I'd like to report a crime. I tried to talk to the police about it in Red Wing and they sent me up here. Apparently, it was out of their jurisdiction."

"Okay, what's your name?" the woman replied.

I asked for a slip of paper and wrote it down along with my phone number.

"And what exactly was the crime?" she intoned.

"My best friend and his father-in-law are attempting to intimidate me and entrap me illegally. They are trying to frame me for a crime."

"What would that crime be?" she asked.

"I'm not sure." I continued, "They are just trying to threaten me."

"Can you write their names on this piece of paper as well?" she handed it back to me.

Just then someone walked into the precinct. I tensed up and glanced backward to see who it was. *Oh good*, I thought. It was a cop. For the first time in my life I felt glad to be surprised by a policeman. Passing me, he entered a long hallway to the right and disappeared behind a heavy steel door.

"We'll look them up in our computer. Hold on a second."

"Alright," I said impatiently.

I walked through the entryway, examining a few bulletin boards and noticed my reflection in an empty glass case. I saw my hat and wondered if they thought it was strange that I was a Michigan fan. I am sure they didn't notice, probably paying more attention to how awful I looked. I checked my appearance on the surface of the glass. I was gaunt with scraggly full beard and clothes that hardly seemed to fit any more. I looked like I was homeless or at best a drifter. My coat and pants were covered in filth from my last few days of landscaping. I had neglected to wash them. Suddenly feeling self-conscious, I tried to straighten my back, turning around to ask about their progress. I loitered near the case and boards for a few moments until they finally responded.

"Well, neither of them has a record and if the crime wasn't recent we can't do much."

"Alright. If you can't do anything, you can't do anything," I replied, giving up.

"Here's a card. If anything else happens call the number on the back."

"Thanks. I will do that," I said, turning back toward the door. "Have a good night."

I waved my hand as I turned and left the police station. The winter air was cold as I stood at the entrance, breathing out crystalized vapors. If they didn't before, they would surely want me dead for what just took place. It was liberating, and despite the questionable danger, I was free of fear. It felt good to be alive. How to put myself outside of their influence for good? That's when it finally came to me.

I drove back to Red Wing with a plan. If there was ever a threat to my life, it would be good to know how to get away or at least to have an idea of what would need to be done in order to escape. I took a back road down a remote valley where I knew a drug dealer lived. To work up my nerve I passed honking the horn and yelling obscenities out the window. I did this a few times until I felt like someone was trying to chase me. Continuing on high alert I pulled back onto Highway 61, weaving through light traffic back to my apartment. When I got in, I turned the television on to a blue screen and wrote a note for any possible intruders. If I hadn't driven by the dealer's house like a crazy person I would have probably been sleeping by now, but this was too exciting to pass up. The note read, "Meet me at the local strip club, XXX" and I placed it on the bed. I then packed a bag and hit the frigid streets.

Driving through backroads I slowly made my way toward the club. The highways were dark and there were hardly any cars out but when I pulled into the parking lot I saw that the place was packed. I somehow managed to get a parking spot by the door. I lingered for a moment when a man smoking a cigarette looked my way. I nodded to him, waited for him to nod back and pulled away. The delusions were making me feel like a secret agent and this random stranger a hidden contact.

Heading back into the night I continued to a small town nearby. I sat in the church parking lot for about five minutes and then pulled back onto the scenic rural route. Further up the road I stopped on the side of the road, got out and peed behind a telephone poll. Why I did this I can't say but it felt right. I then doubled back to the strip club, driving past and turning around in the parking lot of a bar further down the highway. After that I drove the twenty or so miles to the Buddhist

Center, parked a few blocks down the road and entered, shoving my key in the heavy door.

"Odds of evasion, 100 percent," I said aloud, escaping the self-induced manic episode.

"The Lama would be so proud of you," I muttered.

I placed my hand over my mouth, shocked. Someone else's voice was coming out. I had to calm myself down. I sat in half lotus in front of the Buddha statue. I breathed a few mantras to myself and the evil thoughts seemed to fade away temporarily. I felt some peace. A little strung out and worse for wear but at peace. With some clarity I wondered how my life had become so fucked. What was I going to do? How would I get out of this mess? I had no idea. I only knew that I had to keep going.

I made a fresh pot of tea and sat in the darkened gompa for about half an hour. The feeling of exhilaration had passed and now I felt lost. Despite their shortcomings Levi and Anna had been a solid support in my life. Replacing them would be difficult but I knew it was for the best. I quietly sipped and felt the gaze of the Lama from across the room. His portrait was hanging on the wall, a silent reminder of fearlessness and an inspiration. I didn't want to go home but it was the middle of the night.

When I got home, I went straight to bed and was out like a light within minutes. Being unmedicated was dangerous and whether or not a crime had been committed, it was clear to me that I needed help. Sleep was a safety net, guaranteeing at least a few hours of respite from my churning mind.

I woke with the sun in my eyes. Groggy and hungry I made my way to the kitchen for a bowl of cereal. I sat at the table when a strange thing happened. I decided to write jokes about my encounter with a fake hitman and send them to my uncle, as well as the local police department. My unchecked mania caused me to do things like this, and despite my efforts the previous night, it continued. As soon as I had sent the message there was an unexpected knock at the door. Alarmed, I looked through the peephole to see a man who appeared to be brandishing a firearm. He looked like one of the thugs from the Middle Eastern restaurant. What the hell was going on? I was pretty sure he wasn't a hitman but the fact that he could be packing heat terrified me.

"Just a minute," I yelled through the door.

I quickly grabbed my hat and jacket, throwing on my shoes so I could leave quickly. Working up the nerve to go back to the door, I opened it a bit to see a cable guy holding a piece of equipment. Widening the gap, he smiled.

"Are you Jess?"

"No, I'm not. You must have the wrong apartment."

Just then my cat escaped, jumping out into the hallway. The man picked him up and handed him back to me. At that point I realized he might be friendly, though couldn't be sure.

"Is this 306?" he asked.

"No. This is 304."

He began reaching into his jacket for something, hesitated and withdrew his hand placing it back at his side. What the hell was that? I shut the door after he politely excused himself.

The fear had found me again. I needed to talk to someone about it. I stopped at the door and frowned. A safe place to go? There weren't any. Dad was supposed to be working in the valley. I needed him. I had the bag I packed the previous night in my car. Maybe I could stay there for a while. It was clear my condition was getting the better of me. I now felt like someone might actually be after me.

I got in the car and began to drive. It was still morning and people were going to work. The road was more congested than usual though I had no trouble navigating it. I decided to take a longer route on an unknown backroad in order to dissuade any possible tails. Doctor Holland, wherever he was, surely must have been laughing. The client who went against his advice was now lost in a delirium not even Jesus could manage. I frantically searched the rearview mirror for suspicious vehicles.

It took me about forty-five minutes to reach the hidden coulee. The lot where the cars were usually parked was nearly empty. My heart was racing, my breath heightened. My father was the only one who could save me. I put the car in park and stepped out into the February cold. I had no idea where he was on the property, only the urgent need to find him. It was mid-morning and the bottom was nowhere in sight. I could no longer keep firm footing in reality as I plummeted downward. Just then, I caught a glimpse of my father in the distance.

34

I approached my father, ready for conflict. I knew I wasn't supposed to be in the valley and that my appearance in this kind of state was unwanted. The landowner had become ill and didn't need any disturbances. I was about to make one.

"Daniel, what are you doing here?"

"I think someone is after me. Can I stay for a while?"

"No. That's out of the question. Go back home and wait for me to come back."

Like hell I was going to do that.

"Are you kidding? I need you and you won't help me?" I approached him further, raising my voice.

"You're not in your right mind, son. Just go home and we'll talk later."

I jumped back in my car and drove to another part of the valley. He followed in his truck and a low speed chase ensued. I was going the wrong way and he wanted to make sure that I left. I continued deeper into the valley toward the landowner's main house. He backed off before I got there. Now alone, I pulled up the long drive in front of the house. I climbed the heavy wooden staircase, ringing the doorbell at the top. No answer. The landowner was probably bedridden and didn't want any visitors. I decided to leave. Maybe there was a safe place in the city I had forgotten about. I got in my vehicle and turned around. Halfway up the drive I was met by a squad car. I exited my car, my arms in the air.

"Are you aware that you're trespassing?" the policeman raised his voice as he stepped out of the car.

The landowner was well-respected, and they had been quick to respond.

"Yes, I am aware."

"You know, it's illegal for you to be here without permission. I am going to hold you for a few minutes until the sheriff's deputy arrives. Have a seat in the back while we get things squared away," the policeman commanded.

I picked up my computer bag, abandoning my vehicle. Sitting in the back of a police car was something I had never done before and it was awkward. The officer drove me to the barn with the cross where my father had been working and we met up with the deputy.

"Why are you out here today?" the deputy asked.

"I was afraid someone might be after me and my dad must have called you guys," I admitted.

"Right. We are going to have to cuff you."

They put handcuffs on me and shoved me in the back of the cruiser. I couldn't help but laugh as I realized I was wearing a shirt that said, "I'm Russian." Maybe they would interrogate me for espionage. I knew the landowner wasn't a huge fan of Communists and the unlikely wardrobe choice seemed comical. The situation was serious however and I laughed because I was nervous. I didn't know what else to do.

I looked down at the restraints on my hands. They read, "Made in the United States of America." I frowned because the freedom I had enjoyed the night before was gone. I had no idea where they would take me or why my father would feel the need to get the police involved. If there were someone following me it would have been the best possible choice, I reasoned. My dad had disappeared as the squad cars began showing up, most likely ashamed of his son. I felt like I wasn't his son anymore. Maybe I was like Zeke to him, a paid employee who was easily expendable. Didn't he care about me more than that? His absence weighed heavy, as though there was no one left to support me. How could he leave me at my most desperate hour?

I sat in the back of the cruiser, attempting to raise my spirits with the knowledge that I was now safe in protective custody. The deputy got into the driver's seat and we slowly pulled away. He set the radio to a country music station as we drove past the small family farms that dotted the landscape.

I felt a strange feeling of peace. I knew they wouldn't let anything bad happen to me, and maybe this might be the beginning of the happy ending I had been looking for. But I felt helpless remembering Mei. What must she think of me now in the back of a police cruiser? The sense of her watching me was stronger than ever. This was the lowest I could get. But as far as she knew, I reasoned, I was getting on with my life and enjoying it, if she gave me any thought at all. We had been driving for a while when I finally realized where we were going.

The story was taking me back to a destination from my past, the Mayo Clinic in Rochester. It seemed I was finally coming full circle, though this visit would be far from funny. It was a couple of hours from the valley to the large hospital and why they decided to bring me there instead of the local hospital or jail was beyond me. They must have thought I needed serious attention.

I wondered what Doctor Woods would think about this. I didn't have a film this time, though I did have a book on my laptop about the visit. It was an odd sort of predicament, and as the car pulled into an attached garage, I was ushered into the same waiting room where I had been held on my previous visit. I told some of the same doctors that I had now returned with a book, though this time arriving under police protection. It wasn't a joke, and since I was refusing medication, they forced a shot of sedative into my hip. I squirmed and tried to wriggle away from them to no avail.

I put some scrubs on and curled up on a bench in the corner of the cell-like room they used to hold new patients. I requested to see Doctor Woods. They refused.

They were deciding where to put me as I tried to rest. The past few days had been emotional, and unwinding was all I could do to stay sane. They brought me cold vegetarian sandwiches, doing their best to comfort me. I was far from compliant. My experience with Doctor Holland had left me in fierce opposition to any kind of medication, and since I wouldn't take what was prescribed, I was considered a threat.

"I am a Buddhist and cannot harm any living being," I pleaded. "I have taken an oath called the Bodhisattva promise, which states that I must be a benefit to humanity. I would never hurt myself or anyone else."

"I understand," said the nurse attending me. "We have to find out what's wrong, though."

"I told you I was in fear for my life. It may not have been legitimate, but I was scared."

"You need to take your medication, though. We are just going to make sure you do that. If you can promise me that you will, we won't have a problem," she assured me.

"Forcing medication on someone is like forcing sex on someone," I snapped.

She frowned. This was not a stance they wanted people to take.

"Do you have a holistic alternative to chemical treatment?" I continued.

"None exist that I am aware of," she replied.

"Not even if I say it is against my religion to take medication?"

"We need you to be on the prescribed medication," she replied bluntly.

I couldn't argue. I decided to roll over and try to get some sleep. I was tired of wrestling with the nurses. It had been five or six hours since I had been admitted when they finally decided to send me to a different hospital in an ambulance. I insisted that they were wasting tax revenue. Instead of listening they had me strapped to a gurney and carried away for a ride that would cost thousands of dollars.

The voyage to Mankato seemed short and I arrived sometime in the night. I didn't know what time it was, only that the sky was dark. They brought me to my room in the psych ward and shut the door. The space was clean, frigid and dark. The lights had been turned down and there was an orange glow emanating in the window from the streetlamps below. I stood by the pane of glass wondering what the future would hold. My journey had taken me many places and all too often it had been to a hospital. It seemed no matter how hard they tried they just couldn't regulate someone like me. I felt the system had failed. I continued to slip further through the cracks, and they could only shove medicine down my throat to counteract it. I retired for the night pulling the stiff, white hospital sheets over my thin body.

Mid-morning, I rose from the lumpy mattress, finding my way to an empty dining room. Someone had ordered a cheese omelet for me. As I sat eating, I was reminded of Edmund Dantes. I was feeling falsely imprisoned, that I was somehow paying for an imaginary crime. The copy of *The Count of Monte Cristo* I had given Jacob probably sat unread somewhere, and now I was living the story. With Mei as my Mercedes I wondered if I could ever escape from this nightmare. I curiously glanced up as other patients entered the room. Were they victims of these silent crimes as well? It wasn't something you asked about in a place like this. How they got to the hospital was their business and I didn't want to pry. Their sullen, hollow faces told me enough. They appeared almost as ghosts, haunting me in this vulnerable condition. Sometimes when people were unwanted, they would find themselves in places like this, forgotten and lonesome. No one had called for me and I was beginning to think no one ever would.

35

After my breakfast a nurse brought me some soap and a towel. I took a shower for the first time in weeks, washing the dirt and grime off my emaciated frame. I ran the bar of soap over my ribcage, the bones easily visible under the skin. I lathered soap in my beard and across my fuzzy head. The shower was a small tiled room with a white showerhead on a wand. I pressed both palms on the wall and let the water run down my body into the drain on the floor. I spent thirty minutes in the hot water. Afterward, a doctor wanted to meet with me, so I got dressed in a fresh pair of scrubs and returned to my room for a conference.

"The county thinks you are a good candidate for commitment. I can give you some literature on it if you like," the doctor asserted.

"Literature? If I can read and understand literature on commitment, wouldn't you think I am a bit beyond it?"

I clearly didn't understand what she was talking about. I expected barred windows and rubber rooms. She tried to explain.

"If you aren't taking medication, we have no other options."

"It is against my religion," I exclaimed defiantly.

"Is it true that you told the nurses at Mayo that you are a protector of the planet? We consider that to be a delusion, easily treated with a mood stabilizer or antipsychotic."

"No, I told them I took an oath to be a benefit to humanity," I replied, withdrawing a little.

The religious barriers were hard to get over, even more difficult when they misquoted me. Their lack of understanding was making me seem crazy when I only wanted them to know I wasn't a threat.

"I see. What about your book, A Mexican Dream Journey?"

"It's called *My Mexican Dreams*."

They couldn't even get that right.

I continued, "I was offered a publishing contract. Not a very good one but it was offered. Do you want to read it?"

"No. I don't think that will be necessary. I would however like you to read the literature on the commitment process," she replied, handing me the pamphlet.

After the doctor left, I began wetting a paper towel and placing it over the room's video camera. I sat in bed and giggled until a nurse came in to remove it. This irritated them and they warned me not to do it again. I then made a sign for my door that read "He Man Woman Haters Club. Keep Out!" and posted it up using a piece of adhesive from my hospital bracelet. I was hoping it would help them to dismiss me early.

I wrote on a small piece of card, "My uncle is in United States intelligence. My imprisonment could be considered an act of treason," and slid it under the nurses' station door. Of course, my uncle wasn't in intelligence anymore but they didn't know that. I had become the patient from hell, and after 72 hours of torture they agreed to let me leave.

My three days were up and now I would be allowed back into the community. I was miles from home and my family had decided that keeping me in Mankato was my best hope for recovery. They thought that since it was so far from home, I would have no choice but to stay. My relatives had failed me. Why had they abandoned me? When a family member is in trouble you support them, surely. Maybe my parents felt like I was a threat and didn't want the nurses to set me loose in Mankato. They may have given up on me.

I lingered at the window of my hospital room, having a communion with the ice and snow that had gathered on the ledge outside. I felt a kinship with it, as though the tiny flakes were my family now. I heard a faint knock at the door. The nurse informed me that it was time to leave. I walked into the brightly lit hallway where she was waiting for me. Guiding me to the nurses' station she handed me my computer, my bag of clothes, my jacket and my hat. I checked to make sure the ring was still in the inside pocket and pulled out the Karmapa blessing string. I would need all the help I could get.

"Can you tie this around my wrist for me?" I asked.

She took the string out of the small plastic bag, wrapped it around my wrist four times and tied it in a knot. It was a teal ribbon about an eighth of an inch wide. Putting on the coat and hat I felt ready for anything. As the nurse walked me out through the hospital's main door, I handed her a note I had written on a piece of notebook paper, thanking her for taking care of me. The cab was already waiting. It had been snowing for several hours and the roads looked bad. I climbed into the passenger's seat and greeted the driver.

"I have a distance to go. How much is a trip to Red Wing?" I asked.

"Let's see here. They told me you were going a long way. It will be about two hundred dollars one way," he informed me.

"Sounds good. I need to stop at the bank before we leave town so I can pay you."

I didn't bother to explain to him that it would be almost everything I had. He smiled and made small talk about making the drive several times before. We traveled a short distance to a bank on the outskirts of town and pulled into a spot near the door. I walked into the lobby, glancing at the clock. It was about twenty to six and the sun was beginning to set.

I waited patiently in a short line leading to the teller, wondering what my mother would think about all of this. She was supposed to be visiting me this week. I pushed the thought away. Spending such a long time trying to be a good son wasn't paying off. It didn't make sense. I had done everything right and this mess was all I got for it. What kind of son had I become?

I approached the teller and ran my card through. She counted the twenty-dollar bills, placing them in my hand one at a time. I returned to the cab after ten minutes, letting the driver know I had the cash for the trip. The snow was wet and slippery and a few times at the lights we slid forward a few feet when attempting to stop. The cabbie didn't seem to mind, knowing his car could handle it. His name was Vlad and he loved science fiction. We talked for a while about several shows that I had seen an episode of here and there. Doing my best to keep up I humored him.

"When are they going to develop stun technology?" I asked.

"Well, they already have stun guns. What do you mean?"

"I mean like Star Trek, 'set phasers to stun.' Pew Pew! You know? Why don't we get rid of bullets?"

He paused and thought for a moment.

"That is a good question. Maybe because it would cost too much money to put all of the criminals in jail?"

It was a fair point, but I didn't think killing them was a better idea. I felt like an undercover policeman for some reason in my torn jeans and dirty canvas jacket. For all he knew I might have been. He had sandy blonde hair and glasses that he nervously adjusted on the bridge of his nose in the rearview mirror every time he spoke about his Vietnamese girlfriend. He had visited her in her home country a while back and spoke fondly of the culture there.

"In Vietnam it is nice because there is a lot of corruption. If you bribe the right people you can get almost anything you want. It is easy to do, not like it is here."

I raised an eyebrow, and said, "I am not a huge fan of corruption. It is like the government is a concrete block and you are the sledgehammer. All you are going to get after a while is rubble."

"I know what you mean. I am just saying it is nice for a normal guy like me to have those opportunities. In the United States only the rich and well-connected have them."

"Yeah, I know what you mean."

My thoughts drifted away from the conversation as I remembered my uncle. Yeah, whatever, cabbie. Well-connected, my foot. I was the nephew of a high-ranking military official and still wasn't given any special considerations. If I had been in Vietnam those doctors would have been eating out of my hand, but because this was the United States I was being committed. I didn't know whether to be proud or upset. On one hand I was living in a very clean society, mostly free from corruption and running like clockwork. On the other hand, all my cool perks didn't make one bit of difference and the only thing the Commander was really good for was pranking.

I chuckled to myself. Of course, he was good for more than that, but not to someone like me. Maybe he would be better off with a President or the Secretary of Defense. Palling around with me would only spell trouble. I laughed out loud. I was absolutely certain he did nothing but have tea parties all day with politicians and top-ranking military brass. I mean, what could be more important than getting me out of trouble? I kept laughing and Vlad was looking at me like I was nuts. I am not saying that I wasn't, it's just that explaining the situation to him wouldn't make one bit of difference in the end.

"Sorry. I was just thinking about trying to bribe someone in North Korea. It must be like one of those spiral things you put quarters in at the zoo, only the hole at the bottom goes directly into Kim Jong Un's pocket," I continued laughing. "I mean, what kind of suction do you think that thing has?"

He laughed too. Sometimes I had to make things up like this to hide what I was actually thinking. Who needs to know about a Naval Commander anyway? No one, that's who. I had gone my whole life never knowing how powerful he was and now that I knew and actually needed him, he was probably playing golf with that guy who lost the election. You know, there were several of them. Freedom changes things, and he was protecting it. I didn't have a job, a wife, children or anything of real value, except maybe my car. In the grand scheme of things, I didn't matter too much and I was grateful that I had the wisdom to know that. If I didn't, I would have been gushing to Vlad about how my highly decorated uncle didn't give a shit about me. I knew he did, but he was probably off somewhere trying to convince some government official not to torpedo Mogadishu.

We pulled into Red Wing well into the evening. He dropped me off where I instructed, on the side of the highway. I was planning on leaving the city that night but needed a phone charger from the department store on the other side. I walked briskly through the cold winter, my cheeks flushed, and skin tightly stretched. The doors opened by themselves as I headed for the bathroom to wash my face and survey the damage.

I looked like hell, cold and ragged. I didn't need the mirror to tell me I had been through something. Wandering through a store full of items I couldn't purchase was simple enough but deciding whether to have phone service or gasoline was a bit more difficult. I purchased the least expensive charger I could find and continued on foot back to my father's. As I crossed the highway for a second time, someone yelled my name from a car window. I turned to see who it was, but the car quickly sped through the green streetlight. I remember feeling conflicted about someone recognizing me, but easily dismissed the thought. At this point

I didn't even care if it was someone trying to kill me. Death was only another way out.

36

I walked through a back alley behind an abandoned grocery store. I didn't want anyone to see me and slunk through the shadows. My father's house wasn't far from here. I snuck through the trees in the yard to see if anyone was home. Maybe if I waited until he went to bed, I could break in and find my car keys. I had a few good ideas about where they were being kept.

Still hardy from the hot summer's toil, I decided I could walk the streets for a couple hours while I waited for him to sleep. I strolled through the residential neighborhoods, not really caring who saw me now. Before I knew it there was a pickup truck slowly crawling along beside me, my father's worried face at the window. Apparently, the nurses had let him know I was coming.

"What the fuck? You tried to commit me?!" I kicked his door and beat on the window with balled-up fists. "What is wrong with you? You want me to get locked up?" I yelled.

A girl walking her dog evaded us by struggling through the snow in someone's yard.

"Yeah, maybe you'll read about this one day!" I yelled back at her.

My father sped up and I ran after his truck. I had gone only a few blocks and was now chasing him home, jumping through the hedge as he locked himself in the house. I pounded on the door screaming at him.

"Give me my keys!" I yelled.

"Settle down or I will call the cops!" he returned.

I ran down to the small, attached greenhouse and kicked in the door, entering through the basement. He met me on the stairs as I pulled him down and pushed him around the room.

"What the hell were you thinking? I was in trouble and you had me sent to the psych ward?" I pounded on his chest.

"What the hell were you thinking?!" I yelled now, with tears in my eyes. "Give me my keys, I am getting the fuck out of here!"

I chased him upstairs where he handed me the keys. A squad car pulled into the driveway.

"You called the cops on me again!?"

There wasn't anything I could do. I left the house with my hands in the air. When I arrived in the front yard the policeman had his hand rested casually on his gun.

"What's going on here?" he asked.

"Nothing. I was just trying to get my keys from my Dad."

"Did you break into his house?"

"Yeah," I admitted. "I guess I did."

"You understand that is against the law, right?"

"Yes, I understand."

"I'm going to have to ask you to have a seat in the back of my cruiser here," he requested, opening the door and pointing inside the squad car.

"Fuck me," I replied under my breath, lowering my hands and getting in the vehicle.

This was my father's love, and it was tough. He had raised me to be strong, but my will was now too much for him. The officers questioned me and decided to take me to a neutral place for the night. Vincent was the only person I could think of who would be up at this time. They put me in the back of the car and drove me across the river to his apartment. In terms of security I felt exposed by my father, helpless and alone. I couldn't believe my own dad still refused to offer me comfort. The policeman went in first to alert Vincent that I needed a place to stay for the night. He welcomed me with open arms and a confused look. I could tell this was going to get messy.

"Sorry for barging in," I tried to sound like it wasn't a big deal.

"It's okay. Do you mind telling me what is going on exactly? Was that you on the highway earlier?"

I had made a deal with the police to stay with Vincent until sunrise. It was a promise I didn't plan on keeping. I couldn't believe that he was the one who had called to me from his car.

"My friend Levi and his wife's father were intimidating me. In some ways I am taking the fall. Also, I wrote a book." I continued, "Do you want to read it?"

"Sure. I mean, I guess so," he replied, offering me a chair.

"Can you give me a ride to my car? I don't want to sit down."

"You're not supposed to leave, though," he frowned.

"If they catch us, I will tell them I forced you to take me."

He reluctantly agreed to drive me across the river to the landscaping shed where my car was being kept. I didn't want to burden him any more than I already had, and I could tell he was anxious. Unlike my father he had no idea what had happened. The police had brought me to his house and here I was, talking about random people he had never met. Things were getting a little awkward. We drove past the police station in complete silence and I quietly gave him directions as we neared our destination. I jumped out of his car before he had stopped and began brushing the snow off the windshield of my car with my sleeve.

"Daniel, I want you to get help," he yelled out the open driver-side window.

"You might never see me again after tonight!" I yelled back.

"Get help," he reiterated.

He rolled up the window and left me to fend for myself in the frigid February night. I warmed up my vehicle, grabbed the scraper from inside and started chipping away at the ice. Now all I had to do was get out of the city.

I drove to the nearest gas station to fill up. The handle clicked and before I knew it, I was taking an alternate route out of town. Up and around a ridge I would head for Hastings and then turn toward Highway 52 and Rochester on my way south. I didn't know where I was going but I knew that it would be far away and that I wouldn't be coming back any time soon. The only thing stopping me was the snow on the roads, and my car didn't seem to have a problem with that.

Halfway up the ridge a police car crossed my path headed in the opposite direction. I looked down at my speedometer and realized I was going five over the limit. Damn. The cop turned around and flashed his lights in my rearview mirror. My brush with freedom abruptly ended as he pulled me to the side of the road. I couldn't believe that for the second time in a week the police would have me in their custody. *Maybe they'll just give me a ticket and let me go,* I thought. I looked in the side mirror as the officer approached, the exhaust fumes from the car like a veil hiding his identity. As he passed through it, I realized he was one of the policemen from my father's house. That's when I knew I wasn't getting away. He knocked on the window as I searched for my insurance, knowing it would be another long night.

37

The officer told me I would be going to the hospital for a routine checkup. The cruiser pulled up to the Emergency Room and we entered under the large red-lettered sign. The nurse inside introduced himself and placed a red medical bracelet on my wrist.

"Wait" I said anxiously. "You said I would just be here for a checkup."

"Well, they want to keep you for observation."

"You lied to me," I replied, becoming angry.

They brought me to a holding space in the emergency room, close to where I had overdosed. The neutral colored walls reminded me of death. I sat quietly on the paper sheet covering the table and waited for another doctor to perform his examination. After a few minutes a man in a lab coat appeared. He had thinning light brown hair, meagre lips and a face like a clenched fist. I wasn't sure how often policemen brought in patients like this. He seemed to take it in his stride.

"So, what seems to be the problem?"

"The police think I am crazy. They told me I could get checked out and then they would drive me back to my car. Is that true?"

"If they brought you here, they must think you are a threat to yourself or others," he sternly pointed out.

"It is literally against my religion to harm anyone and I don't believe in suicide. I am not sure how many times I am going to have to explain this."

"According to them you have been having problems for a while now," he reminded me.

"That's true. Do you think I can go?"

"No. That isn't possible."

He held up a needle to the light and flicked it a few times as the policeman entered the room to hold me down. For the second time in several days I was being issued a sedative. It only took a few minutes for my nerves to calm. I lay on the table drowsy eyed, remembering the feeling of floating above my body.

"You know, I died of a drug overdose in one of these rooms."

"You don't say…" the doctor looked annoyed.

"Yeah. Look it up in your records."

The policemen led me through the empty hospital hallways to the ward reserved for psychiatric patients. My belongings were locked in a closet and I was shown to a small hospital room with a twin bed that had an impression in the center from so many other patients laying in it. The space seemed to be decorated in the 1970s when yellows, oranges and browns were more commonly used as decorating colors. The curtains were a sickening shade of baby poop yellow and the carpet reminded me of mud. The orderly informed me that I had a commitment hearing the following day, set up from my time in Mankato.

I frowned. This problem wasn't going away. It didn't make sense that I could be falsely imprisoned like this, though I knew there were reasons. I had made mistakes and there were many who didn't like what I was doing. The incident at the police station was reason enough I supposed, and as I sank slowly into ruminations, the delusions caused by the lack of medication took hold.

During my time promoting my film I had sent the video link to several public officials, urging them to do something about immigration. Perhaps one had been in opposition and decided to make me an enemy. Perhaps my father wanted me locked up and out of his life, never to be heard from again. Perhaps Mei found out about my book and had pulled some strings to see that I was silenced. These thoughts floated through my head as I tried to come to grips with what had happened. Clearly, I had gone insane from the lack of food, social support and stress caused by overwhelming debt. I tried to tell myself I would get out of it.

I walked into the bathroom, closing the door and sitting with my knees pulled up to my chest in a corner of the shower stall. I stared up into the vanity lights, which were now behind a translucent shower curtain. I began to cry big wet tears that rolled down my cheeks onto my forearms. The freckles there seemed to have been stained from all my nights of hardship.

"Why are they doing this?" I sobbed, as though someone would answer.

By now my sleeves were covered in mucus and my shirt was becoming damp. My eyes were red, and my head felt shrouded in darkness, like the calm of a warm summer evening with a sky full of shooting stars. It's funny how crying has the ability to do that to a person. Nature's healing was the best kind. If only this illness could be cured by something as inevitable as a good cry. For the time being, the problem was solved. Tomorrow the doctors would begin with their diagnoses, their treatments, their endless pills.

I felt alone on the cold tile floor. No one could hear me there nor did I want them to. I was too tired for shame or embarrassment. Pulling myself up I once again looked at my thin frame in the mirror. Dark circles framed my eyes, my cheeks glistening in the unnatural lights of the hospital bathroom. The fuzz was still growing on my scalp. I felt like the skeleton in someone's closet. The secret I kept was not to be shared, and in a way, I was also locked away. I remembered a young woman named Johanna. What had happened to her?

It was well past midnight when I finally went to sleep. The last thing I remembered was a faint creak as a nurse quietly poked her head in the room to check if I was alright. I wasn't alright but I pretended to sleep, and she went away. The light she let into the darkness of the room played on my eyelids, and as I drifted away, the stars in my mind gave way to pitch black night.

38

I was living with my mother in Red Wing and working for my father landscaping, two summers after my fateful overdose. They had gotten a divorce when my brother and I were very young. It had been a struggle for Russ because he was several years older than me and remembered our parents being together, but I was too young to know the difference. Despite Russ's anger toward my father, he was the foreman for one of his landscaping crews. Ever since my overdose I had been nestled safely under his wing. He had taken care of me after my family realized that I had a drug problem and continued being supportive as I was dealing with the fallout.

Ever since that day in the deer park I struggled with the darkness of my previous actions. I often missed work for weeks at a time and spent all my hours in bed, my body struggling to regain its drive so I could go about my day retaining some semblance of normal life. It was almost as though my extremities were going into withdrawal and my torso was doing everything it could to hold them together. My mind was ravaged by nightmares and confusion. Going out in public was like landing in a war-torn country. I felt threatened by the smallest details and dwelt on them like they were sensitive pieces of top-secret information. Why was that random woman wearing a blue blouse and what did it mean? What did blue represent? Was there some secret language beneath the objects and beings of everyday existence that no one else could pick up on? It seemed like I was constantly being bombarded with information that I didn't know how to decipher, or worse, that only I could correctly decipher, the information being of a dangerous nature and representing an immediate threat to my person.

On a cool June morning I decided that I had the courage to face the day and set out on my bicycle to the landscaping shed about a mile from my mother's house. I was usually early and could take my time getting there. I rode through the familiar streets of Red Wing, half-asleep. It only took me a few minutes to reach the shed and as I hit the gravel parking lot Russ was outside loading tools into the truck.

"Hey Snap, how's it hanging this morning?" Russ called out. He liked to call me Snap for some reason.

"Not bad, I guess," I replied. "What's on the agenda for today?"

"We're hauling the bobcat and trailer to where we started digging out that pond the other day. We will have to stop at the quarry to pick up some stone block as well." Russ continued, "I hope you have your muscles today."

"I can do it. No problem."

I locked my bike to a tree and helped Russ prepare for the day. I could tell he felt bad about abusing me as a child because he bought me breakfast and lunch every day. He was even taking me out to see some live music after work. Despite my childhood trauma and previous drug addiction, I trusted Russ now. He could be a little forceful at times but was a decent guy to his family and most of the people around him.

Russ's biggest downside was his constant need to belittle my father behind his back. He made him look like a joke in front of the other workers and even had me believing it. My father knew it was happening but loved his son more than anything, and so allowed it to continue. Russ was a very hard worker after all. I wasn't far behind him, but I clearly did not have the motivation to run a crew. I could hardly even keep track of my own life.

We worked steadily digging out the pond until the heat from the late morning began to wear us down. At eleven we took a short break. My eyes were closed as I lay on top of the bobcat, my legs dangling over the front of the roof. Russ had gone to the gas station to get us something to drink. I sensed a presence nearby and lifted my head a little. The sun beat down directly into my eyes. I shielded them and squinted to see a young woman with a quiet look and John Lennon glasses staring back at me. I smiled and rested my head back on the roof, reaching into my pocket and pulling out a cigarette from the crumpled pack. I placed it in my mouth without giving her a second look. I wondered what her appearance represented. Who was she? Was she a representative for some other entity who had taken an interest in me? Why had she come? I took a drag and let it creep slowly out of the side of my mouth.

I had not yet begun to appreciate this kind of work and dreaded the break ending. Opening one eye I flicked the lighter. I took another long slow drag off the harsh tarry filter. Russ would be back soon to build walls inside the massive hole we had just put in the ground. I lifted my head again and the girl was gone.

"Come on. Let's go," Russ hollered.

I rose slowly, grabbing the dirty work gloves that were sitting in the bucket of the bobcat. The stone blocks weighed about seventy pounds and for the rest of the afternoon I would be carrying them to and from a foot-peddled manual splitter. Russ measured and placed them and when we would finish a row I would come back with a strong adhesive to complete the job. It wasn't the most glamorous work but the homeowners would feel quite posh when the job was finished. I hauled the block for four more hours before we started packing tools into the truck. Riding home was the best part of the day. The one-ton truck was practically new, with a shiny black trailer for the bobcat. Thanks to Russ and me, my father was almost breaking even. There seemed to be an inexhaustible stream of high-end work. I put one leg on the dashboard as I pulled out another cigarette.

"Another cig, Snap?" he smirked.

Russ chewed tobacco and left half-empty containers of spit everywhere. They were terrible habits but normal for men on a landscaping crew. Banter was commonplace and we often had insult wars that almost always ended with me embarrassed over something Russ had said. Today was no different.

"Snap, that birthmark on your head makes you look like Mikhail Gorbachev."

"Don't you mean Miguel Gorbachev?" I questioned.

"Don't be silly, Snap, he is Russian not Mexican," he replied, laughing.

"It is just a tiny dot. What are you talking about?" I said, pulling down the sun visor and looking at my head in the mirror.

"I am just kidding, Snap, don't get your panties in a bundle."

The one-ton roared loudly into the gravel lot and I hopped out quickly, placing the tools in a lean-to adjacent to the shed. In those days we had a large greenhouse that spanned half a city block. The summers I spent there were some of my favorites. The smell of moss and dirt filled the air and the giant fans produced a constant hum that gave the place a peaceful, calming effect. It appeared that some new employees had started that day. As I walked into the greenhouse, I noticed an unfamiliar girl at the potting bench. She couldn't have been more than sixteen. She was petite with pale skin and dark locks, wearing an oversized work shirt. She looked completely innocent, like a newborn fawn. I walked over to introduce myself.

"Hi, I am the boss's son."

I didn't give her my name.

"Nice to meet you. My name is Johanna," she smiled.

Self-conscious, I did not give her a second look. I wiped my dirty gloves on my shorts and headed back out to the truck. Russ was waiting there with some of the other workers and had a comment about the new employee.

"Did you check out that hot young filly, Snap? She has your name written all over her."

"Yeah, right," I said, embarrassed.

"Why aren't you more interested in girls? I just want you to show a little interest. I know she seems young but who knows? You might have a chance. I can get you her information from my friend."

"No. That's alright," I replied.

"Alright then. I will leave you alone about it. For now…" he trailed off for a moment. "You ready for that concert tonight or what, Snap?"

"Can't wait!" I grinned.

Russ and I gunned it out of the shed and headed up Highway 61 into Saint Paul. At that time, I only had a driving permit and Russ would often let me drive his green 1979 Chrysler LeBaron. I had made a mixtape of driving music and we would cruise around the hills and valleys of Red Wing with the windows down and stereo blasting. It was great to have a brother I could be proud of but Russ's love for fast women and alcohol didn't sit well with me. I suppose I wanted something more from life than just that and judged him for what I took to be a certain shallowness.

The sun was slowly setting behind the city skyline and we were almost to the small venue where we would see a folk musician play. I tried to focus on the road and engage Russ in conversation. I still wasn't very good at multitasking while driving but I figured I would give it a shot.

"Russ, why do you always talk badly about Dad?"

"Well, Snap, he kind of left us high and dry as kids. I would say I have a right to give him a little shit."

He had a point.

"Yeah, but he is only human. He made some major mistakes during the divorce, but you can't completely write him off. Why are you so angry?"

"I haven't written him off at all. I just felt betrayed that he would leave Mom for another woman. You wouldn't understand because you were too young to know what it was like to have two parents. I wish you wouldn't take this stuff so seriously. You are a young guy! You should come have fun with me more often and not worry about Dad so much."

"Yeah, maybe you're ri—"

I was stopped mid-sentence as a small animal ran out in front of the car. I swerved and narrowly avoided it.

"Whoa, close but no cigar," I laughed anxiously.

What did the near miss mean and how did it affect the break in our conversation? Was this some sort of sign? My mind raced as I tried to hold it together. Russ laughed too, a little more wholeheartedly.

"Thanks for coming with me to this concert, Snap. I love that we can spend time together like this. You and I can put the past behind us. I know I made your life hell growing up, but I want to make it up to you."

"Yeah," I replied timidly. "Thanks for the ticket."

"We are gonna drink some beers tonight, right?" Russ quizzed, jabbing at my arm.

"Yeah, yeah. Okay, okay," I smirked.

In the coming months Russ and I experienced a harsh division. Johanna had become an obstacle in our brotherhood and Russ's unwelcome encouragement would lead to disastrous circumstances for me mentally. It saw us at odds with each other for years. Russ moved away and the business entered a new phase. My father would rely mostly on hired help from outside of our family.

I often forgot about the days when Russ and I were happy as brothers. Sometimes the cosmic drama had other plans though. Here in the hospital I was missing him, wishing that things had turned out differently. Had he really set these events in motion or was I just making him the scapegoat? Russ was by no means a one-dimensional villain and deserved a great deal of credit for making me the person I was today. However, his influence had been double-edged; it hurt just as much as it protected.

I read in one of the Lama's books that every good thing that happens to you is a blessing and every bad thing a purification. I had trouble distinguishing which Russ had been. This was my one shot at redemption, and I had to take it. Tomorrow would be the hearing and then who knows what would happen to me. I had hoped it would all be over quickly and painlessly, but it appeared I wouldn't be so lucky this time. I would have to wait and see what the universe had in store for me.

Daniel

39

I awoke disturbed in the morning. The sight of an orderly standing beside my bed brandishing a device used to check vital signs nearly made me jump out of my skin. I was silent as he recorded my pulse and blood pressure. I wanted to scream at him, to tell him to get the fuck out of my room, but I didn't. I knew that would only cause problems for me here. My father was to arrive in an hour or so with a suit and an electric razor so I could shave. This wasn't going to be a happy visit. The hospital room felt cold. Wrapping myself in a blanket I sat in the large windowsill and studied the snow formations on the branches of an evergreen. What would the coming trial bring? The thought that it was a foregone conclusion was burning a hole in my mind. I knew there was a way I could fight this. I just had to figure out how. My father arrived with my suit. He sat saying nothing as I changed in the bathroom.

"You know, they could be doing this on purpose," I yelled out to him.

What do you mean?" he asked.

"Remember that girl who used to work for you?"

"Which one? A lot of girls have worked for me," he said, puzzled.

"Her parents got mad at me for talking to her and I got into trouble. Maybe they felt like I got away too easily."

I straightened my collar, deciding against wearing the tie. The entire situation was similar to Poe's short story, *The Tell-Tale Heart*, where the narrator is driven to confessing to a crime by his tortured sense of guilt. Perhaps somewhere in my subconscious, I was embracing the consequences of my actions instead of running from them. I had opened myself up to the idea of atonement and now the negative karma was flowing out of me and coalescing right here under the judgmental gaze of society. Maybe it wasn't such a bad thing if it would finally see me reset to zero.

"Don't be silly. They forgave you for that," he replied, sympathetically.

"Are you sure?"

"Yes, I am sure," he paused. "Listen, I won't be able to attend the hearing."

I re-entered the room, not quite believing what I had just heard.

"Why not?"

"I have business to attend to. I have to leave in about five minutes."

I felt utterly abandoned. He gave me a hug and wished me luck, disappearing before I could assimilate what had just happened. What the actual fuck? My dad had left me alone again at a time like this.

A nurse appeared shortly after and watched me as I shaved my head and face. As I stared into the mirror I realized, not for the first time, that the only one I could rely on was me. I had to admit I looked good in my black, slim-fitting three-piece suit with a blue shirt that matched my eyes.

I walked with the nurse to the nurses' station where a sheriff's deputy met me. I had asked the nurses to print several documents from my laptop for use in the trial, including a copy of my book. The nurse handed me the stack of papers and a belt. I rolled the lint off my jacket and slacks before leaving with the deputy through the hospital's brightly lit corridors and out to the waiting squad car.

A public defender had been assigned to me; a lawyer being paid by the same people I was to be defended against. Sickness spread through my guts and my breath came fast and shallow. I was about to take on the whole system, to be tried as a criminal who had committed no crime. The odds were very much slanted in the county's favor.

Arriving at the courthouse I followed the deputy up the stairs of the historical building and into a small waiting room where I would meet the defender. She entered carrying a leather bag, containing what I imagined were legal documents. I placed my own documents on the table and looked her over. She was a tall, heavy set woman with glasses and long dark hair. Dressed in a suit with slacks she looked professional enough. But was she on my side?

"Hello, my name is Ms. Jiménez and I will be your public defender. I am here to answer any questions before the hearing."

"I brought some documents for you to look over," I said, pushing the folder over to her.

She thumbed through a few of them. I latched onto the fact that she had a Hispanic surname. Maybe she would read my story and sympathize with my plight.

"And what exactly are these?" she asked.

"It is a copy of a novel that I wrote and some background information about my situation."

"Alright, I will look them over." She continued, "Do you understand that you are being put on trial to decide whether or not you need to be committed?"

"That is what the novel is for. Obviously if I can write a novel, I am not a good candidate for commitment."

"There are varying degrees of mental illness," she replied.

I frowned. If this really was a case about my mental health, she would have to be sympathetic to my situation in order to defend me. Obviously, it didn't matter to her whether I was ill or not, she would be paid either way. Judging by her skeptical comments she appeared to be fighting for the other side. I wasn't paying a dime for her counsel and I appeared to be getting exactly what I paid for.

We exited the room and the hearing began. We sat in simple, polished wooden chairs that reminded me of something you would stand on if you were trying to hang yourself.

"I am still writing novels. This hearing is actually in the third part."

She ignored me as the judge began to read the details of the case. Unbeknownst to me several complaints had been filed against me, noncriminal. Who these complaints were from remained a mystery, and since they couldn't charge me with anything, a civil trial was the next best thing. The date for my sentencing was to be in ten days, after that who knows where I would end up. People's lives were decided on a day-to-day basis in this courtroom and they were shuffled in and out like cards. These trials were not supposed to be gambles though and it was becoming clear that this game had been fixed. The question of where Ms. Jiménez's salary was coming from was foremost in my mind.

Clearly, she didn't care about these things. She saw me as a hurdle in a row of many that she had to jump. If I had fled as originally planned, I would have missed this hearing but that would only have led to more trouble. As always, I counted my blessings. In tough times you can tell who still cares for you because the thoughts of them do not break your heart. The further I got into this mess the more heartache I felt, proof that people were leaving me. Mei was the one to set these events in motion. When she rejected me it destroyed my friendship with Levi. My paranoia about the situation had caused my Dad to turn his back on me. People were dropping left and right. Who was next?

"It couldn't be me," I thought. "I'm not crazy."

The judge's voice reverberated through my psyche.

"The commitment trial will take place in ten days' time, at 10:00 a.m. in this courtroom."

When Ms. Jiménez stood up to leave, I placed my head in my hands, wanting to cry. I remained in my chair, despondent, not wanting to move. A sheriff's deputy appeared in the doorway to the courtroom.

"Come on. Time to go, Daniel," he commanded.

I slowly stood up and followed him back out to the squad car.

In half an hour I was out of my suit and back in my windowsill. I had folded the blanket from the bed, placing it on the cold stone that comprised the ledge. This would be my home for the next several days. I would wait. I rested my fevered head against the cold glass, feeling relieved by the subtle change in temperature. There was nothing more I could do for now except try to convince the defender of my sanity. Given the events of the past several weeks, this was a daunting task. I breathed heavily on the pane and drew shapes in the haze.

At around 7:00 p.m. a nurse appeared at my door and asked if I was ready for dinner. I quietly refused and withdrew to the irregular hospital bed. I lay in corpse pose and stared at the ceiling. "In a few months' time all this will be behind me. It's just a formality," I told myself. "It's just a formality."

Daniel

40

I am crouching in the bushes outside the secluded mansion when our squad leader yells his command into my headset. I'm breathing heavily, trying to gather my courage. I pull a gold ring on a chain out of my fatigues and kiss it. It is my grandmother's ring. I place it back under my uniform and jump to my feet, charging forward, full of terror and grit. An automatic rifle is going off, the shots deafening, peppering the air. I run, firing a short burst of gunfire at my assailant's chest. Dodging more gunfire, I make it to the side of the building and kick the door in. I look left and right. Over there by the window a man in a suit. I take aim, firing a quick three round burst. He goes down.

The room is something else, with lush Persian rugs, a crystal chandelier and what looks like a picture of John F. Kennedy on the far wall. What the fuck? *This place seems familiar*, I think. I run to the large white double doors at the far end of the room, crack them open and use a small tactical mirror to look down the long hallway. Mei emerges from a door further down and runs towards me screaming. She is half naked and terrified. She waves her arms and shouts things I have trouble understanding.

A man with a gun appears. He looks like Levi. He yells, "Get back here, you bitch, or I will fucking kill you right now, I swear to God!"

He raises his weapon. I pull her down and through the door. Gunshot. Pain blooms in my neck. I stagger back. I look down and splats of red are falling, like a preschooler's art project, daubing the expensive carpet. They spell out the simple phrase, "Take the pills dumbass." I am down now. Mei pauses for an instant and looks down at me. Her eyes are wide and staring. She runs out the open door towards the jungle.

I opened one eye and clutched the right side of my neck. I looked around. Only the empty hospital room. Had I ever loved anyone enough to take a bullet for them? What about Mei? In my dreams, apparently, I would die for her. But what about shy, cowardly Daniel? Probably not. Since the overdose I'd been afraid of my own shadow. I couldn't even summon the courage to talk to a girl, let alone die for one. Why had Levi appeared again? He was an enemy now. I knew he probably pitied me, and I hated every second of it. I couldn't sleep. When the nurses came to wake me, I politely told them to go away.

I was still in bed mid-morning, when the county worker showed up. She was a sharply dressed woman in a pressed beige suit coat with a matching skirt, accompanied by an associate holding a notepad. They were here to perform an investigation so that the county would have something on which to base their case, as though they didn't have enough already.

She introduced herself as Janet and did not introduce her companion. They reminded me of the old television show, "Murder She Wrote," and as we talked the quiet one scribbled down the minutes.

"Do you even know what's going on?" I began.

"We are not clueless. Why do you think you are here?" Janet replied.

"Well, I tipped the police to a supposed crime and then thought someone was trying to kill me."

"Do you still think someone is trying to kill you?"

"Well, I don't know. Maybe there never was." Ashamed, I looked down at the blankets covering my waist. I was silent for a moment, remembering my conversation with Doctor Woods. "I still don't know if someone was trying to kill me. I thought it was a cable guy that came to my door," I sighed.

"So, then you can see why you need to be here. I see you are still refusing the recommended medications," she replied, motioning toward her shadow to make a note.

"Yes, but I am taking a little. "I had agreed to take the minimum dosage.

"We consider you to be a threat to yourself, which is why we want to place you in commitment."

They continued to question me about my history, where I went to school, my past drug use and employment. It took about forty minutes. She handed me her card and left, the second woman trailing behind her. I didn't know at the time that Janet would be the woman assigned to my case and that she was meant to be my ally. I had treated her as an unwelcome intruder to my cell-like sanctuary.

I climbed back up into the window and as the hours and days passed, I only left for a group now and then or to the dining room for food. My defender was nowhere to be found. After a few days without a returned phone call I notified the district office that she was giving up on me. They informed me that they couldn't give me a new lawyer unless it was a criminal case but agreed to send a message along with a gentle nudge. I received a call within an hour.

"Why haven't you returned any of my phone calls?"

"You appear to be delusional."

"Why do you say that?" I replied, a little offended.

"You are clearly suffering from delusions of grandeur. What is it you hope to accomplish here?" she countered.

"There's nothing grand about being in a commitment trial. I did what I did out of love."

"I doubt you are in love, more like obsessed, and this trial is not a joke," she exclaimed.

She had a point.

"I plead not guilty. Can you help me?" I begged.

"I will try, but you have to take the prescribed medication."

I still felt that I needed to prove my innocence. My sanity was on trial and I was determined to show everyone that I was not a kook. I had a good head on my shoulders when it wasn't put under unbearable stress from social isolation, financial hardship and complete heartbreak. Anyone would have lost their mind though I would swear on my life that I had found mine again. As much as I hated to think of it, I would even swear on a bible, if it came to that.

The doctor had been asking me to take a powerful next-generation antipsychotic, something that sounded so chemical-laden I dared not ingest it into my body. Who knows what kind of things they put into that small white pill? I didn't want to find out, though if it could help my case, I would reluctantly agree. I told the doctor, a short shrewd man, that he looked like Sigmund Freud. He, in turn, compared me to Edgar Allan Poe, describing him as a poet who wrote of unrequited love. There was nothing lost between us and his presence was as unwelcome as that of Janet, the county worker. We traded barbs daily even though I knew he had the authority to weaken my case.

"If I am committed it will look like you aren't doing your job."

"Take the medicine and we will talk."

"I will agree to take it, but I am a little worried. One of the side effects listed is sudden death. Don't you think that is a little harsh?"

"That is only for people with heart disease. You have nothing to worry about," he spoke mechanically.

"Well, with sudden death as a possible outcome, I'm going to worry."

"Don't. You will be fine."

Several days passed and I had been taking the medicine every evening. I experienced cold flashes, dizzy spells and body aches. The doctor was relentless. I felt as though I had been hit by a city bus, or at the very least dragged behind it for a few hundred yards.

On a particularly cold evening I walked to the dining room and picked up a piano keyboard. I hadn't played in years and felt like it was time. I carried the instrument back to my room nestled under my arm and carefully placed it on my desk. I left the door opened a little so the security guard sitting on the chair outside could hear the lonely songs. Playing the simple melodies, I had learned in my youth, I sang quietly along as my heart became full. An impromptu concert was a rare bird in these despondent surroundings. There seemed to be a song for every love that I had lost, but none for Mei. I hadn't learned hers yet. One song after another, my broken heart parading through the ward.

As though floating on a cloud I drifted. Mei would never experience the peace I felt in these moments, the longing or the bittersweet sadness. I wasn't very good at playing the piano, but my voice was a little better. Maybe my heart wasn't broken. Maybe it was heart disease and the medicine would surely kill me. I didn't even know if I loved Mei anymore, the idea of her becoming hazier as the days and weeks passed. Tracing the outlines of older, more familiar loves in my mind, I felt some comfort. This must be getting over her. It was just sad that it had taken my sanity to get to this point.

After putting the keyboard back, I sat in half lotus on the uncomfortable mattress. I tried to meditate but I was too aware of the nurses staring at me from the video camera in the corner of the room. I pleaded with the Buddha of compassion to take me away from this place, to the meadow, only real in dreams. I sat on my pillow, strained for an hour saying mantras and attempting to create good conditions. This place had become my refuge, my sanctuary and my salvation. It would always be there for me and no one else could touch it. The Lama had once been imprisoned like this when he had returned on a trip from visiting Karmapa. He had faked his own suicide in order to escape punishment, something I could not attempt without furthering my own.

Ignoring the camera, I continued with my mantras. When I had completed one hundred and eight, ten times, I sat back up on the windowsill, watching the people walk to and from their cars. There was little to see other than the parking lot and a few trees, but it was a glimpse of freedom.

The bedside phone started ringing. It was a large rotary phone in a sickening shade of yellowish green. I got down from the window and shuffled across the cold hospital floor to the nightstand.

"Hello?"

"Daniel? Is that you? It's your mom."

"Oh, hi Mom. How are you?" I tried to perk up.

"I am okay. I am more concerned about how you are, though," she replied. "We all thought you were going to take off to another city and lose yourself."

"I am not going to become homeless, Mom. Don't worry."

"How can I not worry with my son in the hospital? Your sister is worried sick about you too."

"I am guessing you haven't talked to Russ," I replied flatly.

"No. Russ doesn't know about what happened. I am not really sure what to tell him."

"Don't tell him anything. I am fine," I snapped. "I have to go. I don't feel like talking right now. I will talk to you later."

"Wait! Why won't you talk to me? Tell me what is wrong."

She sounded sad.

"I don't really want to bother you with it. I know it hurts you to see me in the situation. Why make it worse than it is?"

"Danny..." she paused. "Good luck with your trial. Your momma loves you."

"I love you too, Mom."

Daniel

The phone clacked down on the cradle. I took the sheet off the bed and wrapped myself in it, returning to my perch on the window ledge.

The days stretched on. I was grasping at straws hoping for some miraculous way out that I may have overlooked, but none presented itself. It began to snow, and the flakes melted into tiny droplets that ran down the outside of the window. I watched as they slowly trickled down, collecting more water, gathering speed. My only purpose was to take a pill that made me feel worse. I didn't care about time, I just sat on the window ledge seeking calm. If I could manage that under such dire circumstances, I could handle anything. The snow fell, the water dripped, and I waited. Trying to remain still, I began counting the drops until my eyelids drooped and I quietly dozed. Despite all my efforts at self-reassurance, the trial loomed.

41

The last two nights had been difficult. The dose of medication I was taking had increased and the side effects were hard to ignore. Both nights with extra blankets due to chills passed with aches that left me capable of nothing but staring at the ceiling. The mornings were better once the chemicals had dissolved into my body, but I felt tired and hungover from the wakeful night. The doctor usually visited at around ten o'clock in the morning. He would be greeted by a barrage of insults about the way things were going. This morning was no different, only this time he gave me some unwelcome news.

"Your dosage is going up to three milligrams tonight," he said bluntly.

"Are you crazy? I am already experiencing massive side effects, and this is the second increase in three days. I may be just a patient, but I know enough to understand that twice in that amount of time is much too fast."

"Well, seeing as you refused the treatment when you first arrived, we've had to move the timetable up to get you on the proper dosage before your trial," he informed me.

"What is more important, my defense or my health? It's a stupid question. My previous doctor made a similar mistake and I want to remind you that my life is in your hands," I raised my voice, exasperated.

"Just take the pills and we will get you through your trial," he replied calmly.

"Alright, but I am holding you personally responsible if my symptoms worsen," I warned.

Feeling defeated as the doctor left, I rolled over in bed, wondering if it even mattered. If I truly had an illness what was the point in a cure that made me sick? After the ordeal with Doctor Holland I would have thought a person would only need to go through something like that once, yet here I was with a new toxin and the promise of better health. Double the dosage was one thing; I didn't want to know what triple would do.

I lay on my back watching the smoke alarm blink a dim orange. Outside another patient was having a tantrum. They were lucky I didn't do something like that. Facing commitment anyone would be upset. How many fits had been thrown in this place? The patient in the hall had a dirty mouth. His hollow curses rang round the confines of my room. I longed for home.

This place was on lockdown. Any attempt at escaping was met with restraints and possibly a tranquilizer. The door to my room was open and beyond that there was a heavy security exit that a guard usually sat beside. There was a negative stigma here, as though the people within the institution's walls were infectious. We were that far away from freedom, so close to wellness.

Rumors about my compromised mind would have spread through my family and social circles by now, like a disease. When there was a problem with an abstract and therefore ill-defined concept like a person's psyche, I reasoned, who was to say whether it was healthy or irregular? Show me the person who decides what normal is and I will show you someone who has never known adventure. I will show you someone who has never been outside the box, in fact who doesn't even realize there is a box at all.

In the psychiatrist's mind a person had a place, like a piece in a puzzle that comprised the universe. What they tended to forget was that we had yet to develop a system better than nature, and the only solutions were those created in our own flawed images. The problem was that when people made mistakes the solutions often created remainders, like me. Was I just a number? What were numbers other than abstract concepts we used to describe reality? I felt that using numbers to describe people was as silly as using technical language to describe spinach dip. Humans, I imagined, were not meant to be predictable, and if they were, nothing new or innovative would ever be accomplished. Sigmund Freud was hell-bent on building better mazes when he could have been using the time to make more cheese. I wanted to blame men like him for trying to control things more than the universe had intended them to, even if they were only trying to help.

I put on some socks and wandered down to the dining room where the piano keyboard sat. I played a few notes and then dawdled around reading the signs on the locked white cabinets. Schedules for this and lists for that. I passed by the old exercise equipment no one ever seemed to use. If I hadn't been so depressed, I might have felt like working out. I remembered the time I had spent jogging with Jacob, running from my ghosts in the Mexican dreams. Was this ordeal a biproduct of the nightmares? Could it be I had post-traumatic stress from my imaginings of a real war raging fifteen hundred miles away, or perhaps from a past life there?

I kept to myself for the remainder of the afternoon, sitting in my window and thinking about what had happened to me. Whether a dream or a nightmare, it was clear that I was following something. Whatever it was it seemed to be getting darker and I hoped there would be a light at the end of the tunnel.

"It's okay to be sad…" I said to myself.

I felt comforted by my own voice and it seemed the evil spirits that had been plaguing me were now replaced by my own benevolent soul, comforting me.

"Just hold on a little bit longer…"

I stroked my cheek with my own palm as though it was someone else's. It was like an angel had inhabited my body and was trying to heal me. I placed my hand over my heart and felt pain. I began trying to open myself up to the energy of the universe. I didn't feel like meditating. I just kept my forehead pressed against the ice-cold pane of glass. Against my head it made my heart feel cold, as though it had been broken and I was icing it to numb the pain. I kept very still, attempting to encourage the healing, however, it didn't make the coming conflict any less threatening.

The nurse opened the door at twenty to seven, informing me it was time to take the prescribed medication. Someone had called earlier looking for me. It was Levi, wondering if I was okay. How had he found out I was here and why did he care? I didn't realize at that point what I had done, and that to Levi, I was still a friend. I let the nurse know that I was only accepting calls from members of my family and left it at that.

She handed me a paper cup with three pills and a small container of water. A little nervous, I tipped them back one after the other and waited to see what would happen.

It came on slowly at first, like the world became heavier just because I was still alive. A dull sense of dread filled me. My muscles ached. I knew the benevolent spirit had gone as the pain crept up my spine.

The nurses asked me to sit and watch a documentary about North Korean gymnasts and I felt like a prisoner in one of their political camps. By then my eyes were swimming in their sockets, looking toward the ceiling as my heart began to ache and my toes curled. Was I going into shock? I stumbled to my room and lay down in the bed. I stared into the video camera at the nurses who were watching me being tortured. I saw a cartel thug mutilating my body with some type of rusty metal instrument. This is what it must have felt like to actually be a victim of Mexican drug violence. My vision seemed real – fear, horror, violence, interrogations. Ahmed was the man torturing me. He was being given direction by Mei's father. I assumed they had known each other well from Anna and Mei's close relationship as children. Was he the man behind the scenes pulling these agonizing strings? My eyes rolled back in my head like I was dying.

I writhed in pain for what felt like hours. The tiniest movement set off an electrical current coursing through my nerves. I felt Mei caressing my body, but I wasn't me. I was someone else. Her lips grazed mine. I was her real-life lover, experiencing her passion for someone else. The closeness of her body. My body lay perfectly still as though held in restraints. I went into slight convulsions. I stayed with the pain. I beat my fist on my chest. With each blow the pain intensified until my heart finally exploded with light, filling up red and hot and inflating until my chest could not contain it. It rose up in my throat.

I threw myself onto the floor and crawled into the bathroom. I gave the toilet a hug. It was the worst come down of my life combined with a flu like no other. Was this what Montezuma's Revenge felt like? I stuck my fingers down my throat and vomited. Usually when you do that you feel better afterward but not this time. I did it again and after a second and third time I noticed tissue and blood along with the regurgitated food.

The nurses came and left flat soda and crackers. It felt like I was dying. If I hadn't forced myself to throw up maybe I would have. Antipsychotics were strong. Cursing the doctor, I swore I would sue him. I lay on the bathroom floor for two hours before dragging myself back to bed where I passed out.

42

I awoke the morning of the trial having slept only a few hours. My stomach felt torn and ragged. I had survived, and even though I had yet to stand trial, I felt relieved. I pitied the morning nurse as I threatened her with lawsuits. A man designated by the court was to come and give me an examination later that morning. He was a doctor too and I hoped that his diagnosis would be better than the current one.

I sipped the lukewarm soda from the night before and refused to eat breakfast. I didn't know if I would go to court or not, thinking I would be at their mercy either way. I walked up and down the hallway a few times feeling as though I had been punched in the stomach. It wasn't long before the court doctor arrived to make his observations.

"Hello, my name is Doctor Brown," he began, kindly.

He was a compassionate-looking heavy-set man with wavy hair and smile lines around his mouth.

"Hi, I'm Daniel. Sorry if I don't get up. I've had kind of a rough night."

He pulled up a chair beside the bed, taking a clipboard and pen out of his bag.

I continued, "I have been having bad side effects from my medication and I was throwing up my stomach lining all night. I told the doctor not to increase my dosage again, but he did anyway. I have been experiencing negative symptoms for a while."

"I see," was his only response.

He asked me the usual questions about my background and how I had become a candidate for commitment. Still feeling ill from the night before, I did my best to answer. I told him about Levi, Anna and Ahmed. I told him about graduating with honors and about the book I had written that no one seemed to care about. He nodded knowingly as he jotted down notes.

"Do you know what day it is today?"

I gave him the month, date and year.

"Do you remember my name?"

I couldn't remember.

"Those are all of the questions I have for you. Have a good day and, God Bless."

The last two words were followed by a dead silence. I had told him I was Buddhist and was now wondering if this meant his review would be slanted. Maybe I was just being paranoid, but I thought I knew how these things worked. If you didn't believe, your soul was lost and that might be reflected in his testimony. I found out much later that he was a minister which would in no way excuse what was about to happen. The trial was only a few short hours away and I had put my faith in a man who practiced another religion. Hopefully he would understand my plight and fight alongside me.

Once again, I shaved and put on the same black suit, this time with a tie. When the Sheriff's deputy came, I put my grandmother's ring in my pocket and slid my belt through the loops of my slacks. A little more somberly we walked to his vehicle, and behind bullet-proof glass I rode back to the courthouse. It was March again. "Time to start trimming the grasses," I thought. My father was waiting for me in the lobby. I sat beside him and handed him the ring.

"Can you give this back to Grandma?"

246

"Sure," he said quietly placing it into his coat pocket.

"I'm sorry this had to happen. Thanks for coming and supporting me," I said, not really knowing why I was apologizing to him.

"It's no problem, Daniel."

The County employees working against me walked in and sat on the other side of the room. They were sharing a private joke, unconcerned about my uncertain future.

"Looks like the Babysitters' Club is here," I muttered under my breath.

"What?" My dad looked confused.

"You know, Christians will tell you God will punish you if you do this or that. What they are really saying is, 'we will socially isolate you, judge you and make your life hell.' They use their group think like a magnifying glass to burn you like an ant. I just want to say, 'God didn't do that. You did, you assholes!'"

"Settle down, Daniel," he replied. "It's not like that. There are a lot of compassionate Christians out there."

"Not compassionate enough in my opinion."

"It's okay," he tried to comfort me, resting his hand on my knee.

I was quiet for a minute, gathering my thoughts.

"I believe that karma plays a big role in what is happening. I know you don't believe in it but I hope that one day it will come full circle for us. You have worked so hard and everything is still a mess. Sometimes I feel like I am running in place too," I admitted.

"One step at a time, son."

Just then Doctor Brown walked in and joined the county's conversation. I hadn't realized he was working for them as well. I imagined they were talking about Sunday services. I knew the type of treatment I was going to get. They had a Buddhist in a commitment trial and now they were going to have a little fun with him. I tried to put the thought out of my mind as my defender called my name and whisked me away to another corner of the courthouse.

"So, here is the deal," she said. "You accept commitment and we won't have a trial."

"You mean all this time you just wanted to give up? What the hell have you been doing this whole time? Have you even researched my case at all?"

"Settle down. I am just giving you your options. If you don't agree, you will need to stand trial."

"Do you even need to ask? Of course, I want a trial. I am innocent. You are supposed to prove that, right? Prove my sanity! I thought that was what we agreed on."

A few days ago, she had promised that she would fight for me. I thought it had been set in stone. She was frustrated with my irrational behavior and acted as though being in the court system should have been second nature to me. Things were pretty much predetermined before we even got to trial, so her job was mostly quality assurance. Making sure I made it through with minimal effort on her part seemed to be her only objective. She said she had read the book and the supporting information I gave her though I figured she had probably just glanced over it. I suppose that was enough for a public defender. I walked back to my father, feeling angry.

"Looks like my lawyer wants me to give up."

"What do you mean?" he asked.

"She wants me to accept commitment. I told her we needed to fight."

"Well, that is your decision. I will support you either way," he said. "Your mom and your sister are also pulling for you."

"If I can't talk with her soon, please tell Mom that I'm sorry for not accepting her calls. Tell Jordan I'm sorry for not talking to her boyfriend sooner. I hope it's not too late to get his support."

"No problem. I will, son," he replied. His eyes were full of kindness.

Just then the bailiff announced that court was to begin in a few minutes' time. As we filed in through the sturdy wooden doors, I hoped that maybe, just maybe, this would all work out in my favor. The promise of the American justice system as presented in Hollywood was one of fairness and equality that put truthfulness above all other virtues. Someone had to see that the events leading to this day were set in motion by the mistakes of others, though I was still partially to blame in their eyes. I had stopped taking my medication because I had questioned the ethics of my doctor, leading to the current situation.

Ms. Jiménez and I returned to the same courtroom the hearing had been held in. We waited patiently for the judge to arrive. My father sat quietly in the back of the room.

The bailiff opened the door and announced, "The Honorable Judge Allen Johnson presiding."

43

The judge was a handsome older man with white hair, meticulously parted and combed to the side. He wore a red tie under his long robes and sat with a calm dignity as he heard the opening arguments. The county was accusing me of being mentally ill and arguing for commitment. The evidence was mounting in their favor. The first witness they called to the stand was Janet, my case worker. She swore to tell the truth and took a seat next to the court reporter.

"What is your relationship to the defendant?" the county prosecutor asked.

"I am his case worker," Janet replied.

"And what is your judgement of his mental health?"

"I met with the defendant for forty-five minutes over a week ago. His demeanor was non-compliant, and he seemed delusional and paranoid." Janet continued, "He thought someone was after him and claimed to be an informant."

"Was a crime actually committed?" the prosecutor asked.

"It is unclear at this time if anyone actually broke the law, though a number of complaints have been filed against him in the past two months."

"Would you say he is mentally ill?" the prosecutor replied.

"Yes, I would. He exhibits all the traits of a person with a mental illness."

"Thank you. No further questions."

Now it was my defender's turn. It was time to see if she thought there was anything worth guarding or if she would let the county walk all over me. I fidgeted in my chair, pulling my shirt cuffs out of my jacket sleeves. I had never been on trial before and found it to be more interesting than foreboding. Everyone was wearing their best clothes and acting important. If it wasn't my trial, I probably would have enjoyed the experience, though the gravity of the situation kept me tense. I corrected my posture and Ms. Jiménez glanced at me before taking the floor.

"How long have you known the defendant?" she asked Janet.

"I have known him for a little over a week. When I interviewed him, it was the first time we met."

"And would you say a forty-five-minute interview is enough to gauge the severity of a person's mental illness?" Ms. Jiménez inquired.

"I would say yes. I gained knowledge of his mental health in that time. I would like to remind you that he was also examined by a court appointed medical professional," Janet pointed out.

"You said you don't know if a crime was committed or not. What if my client was just afraid after informing law enforcement? Don't you think that would be enough to cause him to act the way he did?" Ms. Jiménez countered.

"I have reason to believe he suffers from bipolar disorder and was refusing his medication. For him to be of sound mind it is my understanding that he needs to be medicated."

"Are you aware that two doctors have incorrectly prescribed his medication in the past, the most recent being the current doctor at the hospital where he is staying?" my defender pressed.

"No, I was not aware of that."

"No further questions, your honor."

Ms. Jiménez sat back down, and it seemed for a moment we had won a small victory. These deliberations went back and forth however, and it was time to take another hit from the county. The next witness was Doctor Brown, the court medical examiner. He was wearing a yellow sweater vest over a white dress shirt with pens neatly placed and visible in one of the pockets. He had a half smile, the lines near the corners of his mouth becoming more defined as he took the oath and the county began their questioning.

"Do you swear to tell the truth, the whole truth and nothing but the truth, so help you God?"

"I do," he replied.

"What is your profession and education?" asked the prosecutor.

"I am a clinical psychiatrist with a Masters in Psychotherapy and a Doctorate in Psychiatry."

"Did you examine the defendant this morning?" she inquired.

"Yes, I did."

"And what was your impression of his mental health?"

"He seemed scattered and distracted. He spoke quickly and jumped around a bit in his speech. There were several times where I had to ask him to stay on topic," the doctor continued.

"What did you learn about the defendant in your discussion?"

"He works for his father, landscaping, and he attended college in the Twin Cities," he confirmed.

I was a little upset after hearing this. He had neglected to mention that I attained high honors or that I had even graduated. This was awful.

"Did the defendant say anything that made you think he was mentally ill?"

"He told me that when he urinated, he thought his intestines would fall out," he replied smugly.

Now I was really upset. Not only had I not said that, it appeared to be a complete fabrication of the good doctor's own warped mind. I wondered if when he blew his nose, he thought his brains would come out. Telling him that I threw up the lining of my stomach was a grave mistake on my part.

"What would your professional diagnosis of the defendant be?"

"He is diagnosed with Bipolar Disorder though I think more tests might be necessary for me to make any further diagnosis on his behalf," he reasoned.

"No further questions, your honor."

My defender again rose and took the floor.

"Why is it that you say you cannot give my client an accurate diagnosis?" Ms. Jiménez started.

"I have not spoken to him enough to grasp the severity of his illness," he replied.

"What is the chance that you have taken some of his interview out of context?"

"Slim," his only response.

"Do you think his current diagnosis of Bipolar I is accurate?"

"I think his next doctor might want to reexamine the outcome of any therapy or psychiatry services."

"No further questions, your honor," My defender rested her case.

Any ground gained with the first witness had surely been lost with this one. The doctor had lied in order to make me seem insane and to make matters worse my defender had not even made the court aware of this fact, although she could not have been aware of the exact words exchanged during my medical assessment. As he stepped down, Doctor Brown seemed arrogant. I wanted to wipe that smile off his face. The county prosecutor walked over to have a word with my father. She wanted him to testify against me, a request he quietly refused. She returned to the floor.

"We have no further witnesses, your honor."

Ms. Jiménez looked over to me and whispered.

"Do you want to testify on your own behalf?"

I figured I had nothing to lose. I couldn't believe she was asking me at the last minute.

"Sure," I replied.

"If it would please the court, I would like to call the defendant to the stand."

I walked to the front of the room and was sworn in. I felt a little nervous having to speak in front of everyone, though there weren't many there outside of my father and the sheriff's deputy. I adjusted my tie. I sat up straight, ready for anything they could throw at me.

"Do you think you have a mental illness?" the prosecutor asked.

"I don't really like the term illness. I consider it to be more of a mental deficiency that requires medication for missing chemicals in the brain. I use a person with anemia needing more iron in their blood as an example."

"I see. So, you believe that you need to be medicated?" she continued.

"I didn't think I did before but now I see no way around it," I replied.

"Do you consider yourself to be an informant?"

"Yes. Well, a little bit. But I don't think it was for a legitimate threat," I admitted.

"And what were you informing about?" she inquired.

"I don't think that information will be relevant to this trial."

"So, you don't think that it was a serious crime?" she sounded surprised.

"No, I guess it wasn't."

I don't know why I didn't say anything about Dr. Brown's lie. I suppose I was nervous and in a vulnerable position. The testimony of my case worker along with said doctor had sealed my fate. The judge read the verdict. It appeared I would be going to a state-run mental health facility for a month and then a halfway house for three months. For six months I would also be monitored by Janet, my case worker. I looked toward my father and hung my head. I then turned to Ms. Jiménez.

"Thank you. I can be a very difficult man to know." I said, shaking her hand.

I walked over to my father to say goodbye.

"Listen to me, Daniel," he tried to smile with both of his hands on my shoulders. "I want to give you some advice."

"What is it?" I asked.

"Men don't often break. Some go their entire lives avoiding it. They make bad decisions trying to avoid it. It can ruin their lives. I should know."

"I don't understand."

"I know how this has broken you. It isn't the end of your story. Most will not know the strength it will take you to overcome this, but I know you can do it. You have the power to turn your pain into wisdom. When most people are unwilling to be hurt you had the courage. I am proud of you, son."

"Why didn't you help me when I needed you?" I replied solemnly.

"I didn't know how to. None of us did. What happened to you weighs very heavy on me. What happened when you were younger too. I am sorry I couldn't be there for you."

"It's okay Dad. I forgive you," I replied, giving him a hug. "Hopefully I can sell my book and make enough money to pay our debts. This courtroom drama is going to make a good story."

I gave him a sly smile. He smiled back.

"Keep my car safe for me, okay?" I said, handing him the keys.

"I will. See you soon, Daniel," he replied.

Now that the trial was over, I felt a weight had been lifted. Even though I was found to be mentally ill and was given the worst possible sentence, I would be free after six months and not a lifetime. Part of me still wanted to fight it or at least sue the doctors that had taken part. The other part of me was just glad that I would be safe from all the things that had been bothering me. Levi and Ahmed would now be at arm's length with no hope of contact. I grieved for the loss of my best friend, but I also knew that sometimes we all have to move on. Plus, I didn't trust him since his intervention with Mei.

It was odd. I was to be locked up, but I could see the chains being removed. I felt as though I had escaped something sinister. My belongings were packed into the trunk of a squad car as a Red Wing sheriff deputy would drive me to the government-run facility. I tried to laugh with him about urinating intestines though he seemed a little disturbed by the thought. The entire situation had left me with my head spinning and now I could finally take a breath and survey the damage.

I put my legs up in the backseat and let my thoughts drift through the rolling countryside of rural Minnesota. I found some solace in the sight, but this was quickly replaced by anxiety at the thought of the coming months of recovery. What had Doctor Woods said? It takes nine months to recover from an episode like this. Perhaps I should have stayed at Mayo for observation over a year ago. Would it have mattered? It was difficult to say. I brought my focus back to the fields of white taking comfort in the snowy silence of winter.

The sky was clear over Rochester with a few wispy clouds in the crisp air. We pulled into a industrial complex, headed toward the hospital. I was afraid of what I might encounter there but equally fearful of facing my reflection in the mirror. Why did I feel like it was so necessary to be a good person? I felt accountable, judged, but by whom? Had any of my efforts really changed anything? Was I even worth saving? Discouraged, I had many unanswered questions. I solemnly stared out the window at the building that would be my home for the next month. "Here goes nothing," I thought. "Here goes me."

44

The hospital was a pleasant-looking building on the outskirts of Rochester, something far from the rubber cells and barred windows I had been expecting to find. It was my chance to make a new plan and get out of this mess for good. I welcomed the opportunity.

The deputy parked and opened the trunk. I slung my computer over my shoulder, also grabbing two brown grocery bags filled with books and my bag of clothes. He rang the buzzer and we were both admitted through two securely locked doors. *There's no turning back now*, I thought, as if I had a choice. I entered a small room where I removed my suit and put on scrubs. Having skipped breakfast and lunch due to my battered stomach, I was getting hungry. Amid the growling I would have to take some time to respond to questions from the doctors. Opening inquiries like this were usually straightforward. The real questions would take weeks or months to answer and I had nothing left but time. A nurse led me to a small office and asked me to sit down. She then offered me a snack. I ate some graham crackers quietly, not really making eye contact. Shortly after, the doctor who oversaw admittances appeared. He seemed exhausted but was in good spirits.

"It says here in your notes that you have been hospitalized six times. Does that sound accurate?" the doctor began.

"Yes, it does," I stared down at the ground.

"And the first time you were twenty years old?" he continued.

"Yes," I sighed. "I tried to commit suicide."

"Oh?" he sounded surprised. "And why did you do that?"

"I had been having some mental problems for a while. I was having withdrawals from doing drugs and staying in bed for days on end. I felt like I had survived a nuclear war. There was a girl who worked for my father. My brother convinced me to talk to her and she was underage. I think she was scared. I wasn't in my right mind. Her parents were pretty angry at me for communicating with her and had a sheriff's deputy come talk to my mom about it. At that time, I lived with my mom. Shortly after that I swallowed an entire bottle of Aspirin. I was throwing up for hours, but I just got sick. Obviously, I didn't die."

I didn't normally open up to doctors like this. I guess I felt like I didn't have anything to lose.

"That is a little more information than I needed, but now I am curious. What did you say to her?" the doctor asked.

"My brother had convinced me that she loved me, so I told her that I loved her back. I can't remember exactly what she said but I know she questioned my motives. I told her that if you love someone, and it's mutual, you don't have to force anything. I told her love isn't rape. I didn't even realize what I was doing. It was almost like someone else was typing the words in the email. I guess I would have been scared too."

"I see," he replied. "What happened after that?"

"I was in and out of hospitals for a while. I ended up going to college in Minneapolis some years later but had a complete mental breakdown after one year and moved back to Red Wing. I worked for my father for a while, eventually going back to the Twin Cities to finish my degree. I did very well in school and then got a job working in an office. Then I started having strange nightmares and they caused a severe manic episode. Around that time, they changed my diagnosis of

Bipolar II to Bipolar I. After that I moved back to Red Wing and then this psychotic breakdown happened. I am just glad to be out of the courtroom."

"Yes, I see that last one here in your notes. It also says you wrote a story about it. You seem like an interesting case, Daniel. I just have one more question." He continued, "What does recovery look like to you?"

"Honestly, I just want to feel like I am a good person for once. It seems like no matter what I do I am always haunted by my past. No matter how good I become I feel like I am still not enough. Maybe it's some kind of complex. If people have forgiven me, I want to feel forgiven. I can't keep carrying the weight of the world on my shoulders like I have been these past few years. It just isn't sustainable for me. Maybe if I could somehow figure out how to forgive my brother Russ, I could finally forgive myself for becoming the monster I think I am," I confided.

"Well, I don't think you are a monster. Don't be so hard on yourself. This might not be something we can help you with during your time here. Maybe we can get you pointed in the right direction though," the doctor smiled.

"Thank you. I think that would be great," I replied, trying to smile back.

I couldn't help but think of Johanna. This entire time I felt like I was a great guy that no one really thought about or recognized, but in reality, I was just trying to escape this creepy part of myself who had talked to an underage girl. Ever since our communication I always had trouble with women. I couldn't remember how to interact with them romantically in a healthy way. The pain and guilt clouded my mind and caused me to act out. All I was left with now were what ifs. What if my brother had never given me Johanna's e-mail? What if he had never abused me? What if I had never done drugs or become suicidal? Where would I be now? And what about Mei? Why was any of this happening? It was clear the grief and shame had triggered my mental illness. I knew it wasn't healthy to think too much on these matters. All I could really do was acknowledge the regret. I had to forgive Russ. I had to make it up to Johanna somehow and I needed to understand that I could not change the past. I could only move forward.

Afterward a nurse led me to my room. It contained a bed, a short chest of drawers and coat closet. My computer had been locked up but I still had the two paper sacks. I placed them on the bureau, pulling the books out one by one and either setting them in a drawer or stacking them on the surface. I sat on the bed for a long time afterward, trying to process the events of the past three months. Having sent my uncle a message about a story yet to be written, it was time to put it down on paper. The empty notebook was laying on top of the dresser with the rest of the literature. Maybe I'll start tomorrow, I thought, lying down. Tomorrow sounds good. I pulled the sheets up around my neck and slowly drifted off to sleep.

I wake in the extravagantly decorated bedroom. The bed with the silken sheets is still here but Mei, who has been straddling me, has vanished. The door is open. Single shots ring out followed by short bursts of semi-automatic rifle fire. I sit on the edge of the bed and light a cigarette. I take a few slow drags and wonder how I have managed to squander this life of ease and security. Was being in a drug cartel really such a bad thing? We were only providing a service to those who were after a good time. Hell, we were even helping people cope with pain. Of course, there are some casualties involved but what business doesn't have a certain type of casualty? Even corporate offices have remainders, after all.

I stand up and walk to the window. I look down at the courtyard. There is a soldier in fatigues standing watch at the side door. He quickly backs away as a scantily dressed Mei runs past him screaming. I can hear her screams above the gunfire. She almost makes it into the jungle when she is caught by a second soldier who blocks my view of her. I take another drag from the cigarette. The smoke burns my nostrils and the back of my throat.

Suddenly, there is a loud bang accompanied by a blinding flash. It is so bright, the way I imagined God would look. I look for my gun. I fumble to the dresser, partially blinded, and open a drawer. There is a toy gun inside with suction cup tipped foam darts.

"Fuck," I scream. "I've been nerfed!"

"On your knees, motherfucker!" a Mexican soldier yells.

I kneel, still having trouble with my sight. Two soldiers enter the bedroom. It takes them a moment to notice me down on the ground at the far end of the room. There is no "meet my little friend" this time. They have won. There is a sense of peace in all the urgency. I feel free.

A soldier rushes up behind me and hits me in the back of the head with the butt of his weapon. I slump to the floor as everything goes black.

I rolled over in bed and heard the door creak open. I made myself look like I was sleeping as a nurse poked her head in. I suppose she was making sure I wasn't trying to hurt myself. Shockingly enough, after what happened to me, I had no intention of ever hurting myself or anything else ever again. I would surrender to the universe and find my own peace. I would find my freedom.

45

I woke early the next morning to be greeted by a warm breakfast of waffles and a hard-boiled egg. These meals were catered by a nearby prison and it was obvious that the quality of food at the hospital in Red Wing was better. The ward itself was like an old folks' home, complete with quiet rooms and a ping pong table. I smiled, happy that the other residents weren't completely out of their minds, though a few seemed close. One man in particular walked the halls talking to himself about the Mayo doctors. After breakfast I walked past him in a t-shirt with Tibetan writing on it.

"What are you, a Muslim?" he asked. "I believe in God's son."

"No," I muttered. "Actually, I am Buddhist."

"Oh, so you are a Hindu Muslim? You don't believe in God. You're going to hell."

"I like Jesus just fine and I don't necessarily believe in hell," I replied, annoyed.

He was in his early twenties and looked like a gangbanger. I swerved him.

"The Mayo doctors don't like Muslims!" he continued, taunting me as I snuck back into my room.

I took the sheet off the bed and folded it into a rectangle, placing it against the far wall. I sat down with my legs crossed, saying mantras for the rest of the morning. The nurses poked their heads in every now and then, probably feeling intrusive with me sitting on the floor in intense inward focus. Opening my eyes, I assured them they were not disturbing me and felt peaceful for the first time in several days.

After lunch I requested a pencil from the nurses' station. Flipping over my garbage can I sat at the bureau like it was a desk and began scribbling down the second and third parts of my story. For days I wrote, walking the short distance to the nurses every fifteen minutes to sharpen the pencil. Every day or two I needed to request a new writing utensil and after three days they brought me a chair. Each night I lay in bed reading the pages back to myself and chuckling lightly at my own misfortune.

Two weeks passed and soon I submitted two notebooks with "Part Two" and "Part Three" scrawled on the front to my doctor. Since the misadventure with the antipsychotics at the hospital in Red Wing she had changed my daily regimen back to the original medications prescribed by Doctor Woods at Mayo. I was happy to inform her that these pills induced no side effects and I was finally sleeping better and gaining strength. The food was also causing me to gain the weight back that I had lost, and I was looking healthier by the day.

The doctor was a middle-aged woman with the warm smile of a kind aunt. She had asked me to simply call her Caroline. Every week I met with her to discuss my health and thoughts of the previous seven days. We were making a plan and it had never occurred to me that I could include and exclude people as I saw fit. I decided to keep my family members closest, like my parents and my sister, instead of friends who now seemed distant. I worked with the staff on a meditation and exercise routine that got me back into the flow of everyday life. It didn't matter anymore that I was in debt, that I was losing my apartment and that my career was in ruins. I knew I could bounce back and finally get things straightened out if I kept the people I trusted close and gave it enough time and energy. Recovery is a tricky thing, like planning a voyage without knowing what to expect along the way. All you can do is learn to be prepared and take the journey one step at a time. At least that's what I told myself.

That night, I imagine, my doctor paged through the ramblings of the new patient, probably wondering why on earth anyone would want to write a novel in a mental hospital. Plenty of authors had done it, creative minds making up the lunatic fringe of society. I tried to remind myself that a lot of people went through these difficulties and came out better on the other side. My hand had gotten sore from all the manual work and the lapse in dexterity made it difficult for Caroline to understand my chicken scratches.

Some members of staff were curious about my writing but kept their distance because I wasn't staying long. The goal was to stabilize and not to worry myself with literature. After I was done writing I took a break to fall into their groups on reducing relapses. The other patients seemed average and some days gathered in a courtyard outside the facility to play basketball. It was still March and quite cold.

The ice and snow made the ball hang like a dead weight in the air. One of the girls who thought I had pretty eyes was curious about my religion. She finally worked up the nerve to ask about it one afternoon.

"So, you are a Buddhist. What exactly does that mean?"

"It means that I believe in reincarnation and enlightenment," I smiled a little.

"Can you still sleep with women? I thought Buddhists couldn't do that," she inquired.

"Lay Buddhists can. They aren't very common in the United States though."

"Oh..." she trailed off. "So, what do you think about me?"

"You're nice enough, I suppose."

"Hah, what kind of complement is that?" she smirked.

"A half-hearted one, I guess. It's all I have left in me. Sorry."

She looked concerned.

"I think you would be a lot happier if you believed in Jesus, don't you think?"

I frowned at her.

"I don't really think that is very relevant. A lot of people who believe in Jesus aren't happy. Maybe if they actually followed his teachings they would be."

"What do you mean?"

"Like love thy neighbor. Treat others as you wish to be treated. The guy had no qualms about healing those he disagreed with as a means to change their minds. He didn't chastise them. He used compassionate action to enlighten them."

"Oh…" she trailed off. "Well, my mom wanted me to give you this."

She handed me a small pamphlet about Jesus and his mission.

"Thanks. I think." I gave her a confused look.

"Okay, well, I hope you feel better," she said, leaving me to go to her own room.

Later in the week we had a meeting in which the nurses told us not to get into too many personal discussions. They brought disputes to the quiet ward and we would be together for so little time anyway that it was hardly worth the effort.

The second and third parts of the story were by far the most difficult to write and I had already been in the hospital for weeks. It was all still fresh in my mind. Seeing things clearly for the first time, the delusions seemed to fade away. I had acted irrationally, to say the least, though these actions spoke volumes about my disorder. I had written into the night about policemen and deeds that I may never atone for, at least not in this lifetime. It wasn't really true that crimes had been committed so punishment wasn't justified for anyone involved. I only knew that I was imprisoned in a glossed-over jail and that the only way out was compliance. I didn't mind since I was feeling better, though there was an air of vengeance in my writing. I didn't want these indiscretions to be left unspoken. I also knew that I wasn't necessarily the hero. I just wanted it to be honest. When I had written the last word of the story, I had marked the end with a period and closed the book. It was time for me to move on.

46

It was a quiet night at home. I brewed myself a cup of decaf coffee and sat down at my laptop. I was still working at Lacroix and was just beginning to have trouble with my office life. I turned on a messaging client looking for signs of Mei. She was there, as always, though whether she would actually respond was the question. I didn't know what she was doing on the other side of my computer, but I figured it was important. When we spoke online it was in short, interrupted sentences so the conversation was stilted and open to interpretation. The last time we spoke she had just gotten the news that she had a failing grade and so for the past few days I'd been wondering if she had been able to remedy this. For some reason the idea of Mei failing at school troubled me deeply. I hoped fervently that she would respond tonight.

"Mei, you there?"

"Yeah, I am here. Just doing some work."

"How are you doing?"

"Well, I am a little upset with my boyfriend."

I stared down at the keyboard for a moment. She had a boyfriend? "Why is that?" I asked.

"He doesn't look at me. It's like he isn't interested in me or he doesn't want me."

"You wouldn't have that problem if it were me! You are amazing. By the way, did you get your grade up?"

My eyes were tired from the glare of the screen. I squinted at the pixels. Would she pick up on my compliment? Would this be a breaking point in their relationship? *She must like me,* I thought.

"That's what I am working on."

"Oh, how's it going?" I typed out, disappointed she hadn't acknowledged my advance.

"The professor gave me some extra assignments so I will be able to raise it."

"Great. You were always so good in high school. I would hate to see that all be for nothing."

"Daniel, you don't understand what it's like," she had taken a long moment to reply.

"What do you mean?"

"I got the 'F' because I cheated in college and didn't understand the new material."

My mouth hung open. I couldn't believe what I was reading.

"What? Are you kidding??" I pounded on the keys.

"No, I cheated. We all did sometimes..."

I awoke, startled. Was I remembering this or was it a dream? I ran my hand across my balding scalp, worried. If it was true, I wanted to help her cover it up. The first book, the crazy emails and tipping the police about Ahmed, all a distraction, a cover, hiding the real truth. Was this whole ordeal some clever scheme Mei devised to make the idea of her and her friends cheating sound crazy? I put my head in my hands. Was I now an accomplice? I didn't know what to think. I looked across the darkened room at the closed notebook. *Maybe it should stay closed,* I thought. I was ruminating, torturing myself with thoughts of Mei in trouble and why? Because I refused to cover it up.

I went to the common area of the hospital and sat at an empty dinner table. I didn't want to think. In fact, I never wanted to think again if it meant I had to choose between my own peace of mind and someone's reputation. I pushed the thoughts away. A nurse brought me a cup of tea. The familiar smell calmed me, and I took a sip from the steamy mug.

There had to be some other option. What I needed was advice, advice from someone like the doctor. She knew about Mei and that I had loved her, but she didn't know about this. Lies were like cracks in the sides of a building. Covering them up didn't make the walls any stronger, it just hid the lack of structural integrity. What I needed was more support, not more corruption. I asked the nurse for a piece of blank paper and a pen. I quickly wrote my request and folded it in half.

"Can you give this to the doctor?" I asked.

"Sure thing. I will put it in her box, and she will get it in the morning," the nurse replied.

I glanced over at the television on the wall in the common area. Images from the Boston Marathon bombing flashed on the screen. It felt good to be safe and for now I wasn't really worried about the world at large. I was only concerned with my own dilemma, which seemed small by comparison.

"Thanks," I smiled, slowly shuffling back to my room.

I felt more at ease, though the dream's possible basis in reality made it hard to sleep. All these dreams, were they visionary, predictive? Or did they build on information from the past, unlocking its mysteries? Could I really have forgotten such a vital piece of information? It was true that after my drug use my memory was impaired, I had trouble remembering what happened yesterday or the day before. This was important though and I could usually remember significant events. Was I so crazy about her that I had simply overlooked a few lines of text on

273

a computer screen? I spent the rest of the morning watching the sun slowly light the room, lingering in bed a little longer than usual. This development was a snag in my rehabilitation, a relapse into obsessing over the details of Mei's life that needed to be quickly resolved or averted.

I sat mutely through another group on a topic that had already been discussed twice. Each day was like Groundhog Day, but this one, although on the outside resembling all the others, came with a stark, simple choice concerning my future. On one hand, publishing my book could bring my struggling family out of debt, but on the other, the lives of several individuals could be destroyed consequently. Maybe if I changed all the names and obvious indicators, I could avert this potential calamity. The real characters who peopled my imagination could carry on with their lives under cover of anonymity and that way I would keep myself out of trouble. I had been through hell and now it was time to decide. I could try to publish it and see what happened or live a quiet life as a penniless nobody.

"Daniel... Daniel... Daniel!"

"Huh?" I snapped out of my daze. The entire group was looking at me.

"What do you do when you feel your symptoms are getting worse?" the group leader asked.

"I meditate or pray... or whatever."

I would have to think for a long time in order to make sense of it. I wondered what Jacob, or the Lama would do at a time like this. Their counsel would have been appreciated but I was stuck in a glorified holding cell with no access to a phone or the internet. After the group was over, I wandered back to my room and patiently waited for Caroline. There was a quiet knock on the door late in the afternoon. She let herself in.

"You left me a note saying you wanted to ask me something?" she asked, approaching me in a careful way.

"Yes, I woke last night after possibly remembering something".

"That does sound interesting," she continued. "What happened?"

"Well, I am actually trying to decide if I should write about it or not. You know Mei, the girl that I wrote about?"

Caroline nodded.

"She went to an Ivy League school and confided in me." I continued, "She told me that she cheated. In fact, she told me a lot of her classmates did too. At least I think she did. My memory is so bad these days that it might have just been a dream. Isn't cheating at a school like that a crime?"

"I see. I don't think it is a crime. Is this bothering you?", the doctor inquired.

"Yes, I feel like I shouldn't write about it. I am worried about what it might do to her. I don't even know if it is real."

"Maybe you shouldn't then, if you don't know."

"Yeah, maybe I shouldn't..." I trailed off, suddenly distracted. I continued after a moment, "It just makes me feel like people were expecting me to kill myself. Clearly, I had other plans."

"Well, don't jump to any conclusions. This isn't a conspiracy. I am sure this woman had no ill intentions toward you. You are still recovering from a serious psychotic episode so I can understand that you might be a little confused about what took place."

"Yeah. I guess I was just confused because the dream felt so real," I confided. "It had elements that I know were true and others that I am not sure about. I guess I just feel shattered because my hopes were dashed by her. She was what I had been working to accomplish. She was the person I was trying to impress with my studies in college and though I was mostly unaware of it, I feel like she was encouraging me to move forward with my life. If it wasn't her then who could it be?"

"I'm not sure, Daniel," Caroline replied.

"I even cheated once in seventh grade Spanish class," I continued, frowning. "I wrote some of the words on a little slip of paper and hid it under the desk the day before. I guess that is a little different," I paused. "It is definitely the truth though."

There was another slight break in the conversation.

"I could have killed myself," I confided.

"I know it was hard for you, but I don't think you have anything to worry about," She gave me a sad smile. "Do you still feel unsafe? Do you feel like anyone is trying to hurt you?"

I grimaced.

"I am really questioning what is real and what isn't. I feel like it all stems from my brother abusing me. I remember being in my room, never knowing when I was going to be hurt. I feel like that now, like pain could come at any time. It could be Russ. It could be my friend Levi. It could be Mei, the girl from my dream. It could come at any moment. That's why I felt like someone was going to hurt me, why I thought people were trying to kill me. Whenever things should be going well in my life, I devise some threat. I can't just be normal. I always have to be scared."

"You don't need to be afraid anymore, Daniel. It seems like you could have a little PTSD from your past experiences."

"PTSD?"

"Yes, possibly. I am going to add it to your chart."

"There is so much wrong with me," I frowned. "I just really hope that someday I can move past all this."

"I very much hope so too." she paused and looked down at her watch. "I have another patient meeting I need to get to. If you want to talk again, let me know. It's time for dinner, so please go eat. I wouldn't want to keep you from that. Try to get some rest."

I felt so broken. I didn't know how I could ever heal. I also felt paranoid about Mei, still thinking it was some kind of game, because I would never really understand the complete truth. I could only guess regarding what was real and what wasn't in this particular situation. Maybe this was just the way the world worked, where the affluent and important got what they wanted, and the less fortunate were left to pick up the pieces. Perhaps Mei's reputation was more important than mine and I was just an easy garbage bin to hold her indiscretions. That at least made sense to me.

I thought about the Commander. What was his role in all of this? Was I being tortured by some unseen force to make him suffer? Were members of the Chinese government targeting me and if so, was I nothing but a pawn in their twisted game? Was it the Mexicans? The drug Cartels? I knew that the Chinese were trying to eradicate Tibetan Buddhism. I thought on that for a long while. Maybe these groups knew who the Commander was and that I could be used as a bargaining chip for them to get what they really wanted. Perhaps it was the victims of drug violence attempting to speak to me from beyond the grave. Were they trying to get his attention to inspire him to act? It's like I was caught up in some sadistic spider's web. What the hell was really going on? Who was behind all of it?

I sat in total silence for what seemed like hours. I knew it was insane. Could it be the truth? The Commander gave me no special consideration. No phone calls. I was absolutely certain it was in sharp contrast to what would happen overseas. I took comfort in that for some reason. Placing my head in my hands I stopped myself. How could I exist in a world where these things might be true? How could I survive? I must be crazy, I thought. I remembered Mei. I remembered how she was in school. Kind, beautiful, brilliant. I loved that about her. I knew that part of her was still there somewhere. It had to be. Despite all these wild delusions she grounded me. It seemed those thoughts were good for something.

"Daniel," I muttered to myself. "Thinking these thoughts about other ethnic groups is what racists do. That is definitely not who you want to be."

I stood by the window for a long moment, solemnly watching the spring rain drizzle on the cars in the parking lot. I hugged my torso and leaned closer.

"Get a hold of yourself!" I breathed out loud. "Get these silly thoughts out of your head!"

I unwrapped myself and placed my hand on the glass. It was cold. I felt these circumstances were making me into a prisoner in my own country. Thinking more clearly, I only had myself to blame. I needed to be smarter. I needed to be stronger. I needed to remember the man I had become and learn from the incorrect actions taken by the person I was.

A nurse opened the door and poked her head in.

"You don't want dinner?" she asked.

"No," I shook my head. "Not tonight. Thanks."

"Well, if you get hungry just come see me."

"Okay. I will."

The remainder of the evening passed uneventfully. I left the notebooks undisturbed for now, deciding instead to spend the night meditating. I sat on the cushion, attempting to read my lifelines. Perhaps a simple life was all I could afford. I would take the notebooks, tear them up and watch them float down the mighty Mississippi.

I studied the bumps in my prayer beads. They were made of the seeds from a bodhi tree. This type of tree was renamed for the Buddha after he reached enlightenment under its branches. Bodhi was a word synonymous with attainment. They smelled like baking cocoa and I didn't know if it was from the seeds or the oils on my skin. With these beads in my hands I sometimes felt that I had discovered a kind of wisdom and the means to enact it. However, the satisfied feeling often vanished as I was left with the constant questioning about Mei, worries about the prophetic nature of my dreams, about where my life was headed, about my family, money, the book, what I was going to do when I got out of this place. I knew that any good Buddhist monk would put the matters troubling me behind them and move on to other things.

I wasn't a monk though. I could never be one, although it was doubtful whether being a monk automatically meant you were enlightened. I had to get some sleep, in spite of my conflicted feelings. I stood and stretched, turned off the light and curled up in the blankets, reminding myself of the cat who I hadn't seen in months. I was grateful that my Dad had agreed to take him to his house to care for him.

In the morning a nurse notified me that Janet would be visiting that day to talk about discharge. I wasn't looking forward to our conversation and the hospital social worker was out of the office so I would be alone. I went through the motions with breakfast and groups and soon it came time to talk about leaving the small institution. She arrived with an intern learning the ropes, inquiring if it was alright if she observed. I hated when people asked questions like that, as if it were my decision. What was I supposed to say, no? I agreed and we were led to a private room away from the other patients.

"Daniel, I don't want to be your enemy here. I want to help," Janet began.

"You'll have to forgive me. When someone testifies against you, it makes it a little difficult to have a working relationship with them."

She flipped through the pages on her clipboard. The intern silently watched and took brief notes.

"Don't be silly. We can work together," she argued. "Let's see here. It says that you have already made a discharge plan with the doctor here. You'll be admitted to a halfway house and then to your mom in Duluth. Is that correct?"

"Yes, that sounds right."

"And you already have a house picked out. You have been accepted and will be transferred in a few days?"

"That's true," I replied.

"Huh," she continued. "Looks like I don't have much to do with you here then," she said, seeming disappointed that she could not do more.

"We have been working hard on these plans. The doctors and staff have been very good about allowing me to give input. I am very grateful for them," I smiled.

"Well, great! We both wish you success in your recovery."

Several more tiresome days passed on the ward and then it was time to leave. The delusions had slowly faded with correct medications and the passage of time. My mind felt more peaceful. I filled two duffle bags with all the things I had accumulated, one for clothes and the other for books and documents. Some of the more sentimental patients wanted hugs and offered words of encouragement. Wearing my suit for the third time, I stood at the nurses' station with my belongings at my feet. They slid my computer and walking papers over the desk as well as a plastic bag full of loose change and other personal effects. I lingered there for a long moment, not really knowing what to think. This chapter of my life was over and all I had to show for it were massive internal scars along with a knowledge of mental health coping skills and sprinkles of Buddhism. There were also the notebooks, something I wasn't sure I wanted people to see. It wouldn't matter though. At least not for now. For the second time I was a new man, ready to make his way in the world.

I crossed the threshold of the two massive magnetically locked doors and threw my belongings into the trunk of another waiting squad car. I was on my way to West Saint Paul where I would start my life once again. The halfway house was near Cesar Chavez street and I looked forward to visiting my memories of more innocent times there. Three months did not seem so bad and this time I was getting some monetary help from my mother to start a new life. She was even allowing me to live with her while I got back on my feet. I couldn't think of anything I would rather be doing.

As the squad car pulled away, I began to doze off in the back seat. I had been spending a lot of time in police custody and I looked forward to my imminent freedom. Maybe someday I could forgive those who I felt had wronged me and start over again where I had left off. Maybe they would understand my erratic behavior once they heard my version of the story. Just maybe.

I wouldn't wind up with Mei in the end. This is only the place where the camera pulls back to show the police car driving away, further and further until it is just a tiny spot on the highway. What now? Where would I go? The music begins to play, and the camera holds the scenery for a few moments before the screen goes black. What would I want to tell the viewers in the moments that followed? I suppose the most hopeful thing I could think of:

To be continued...

Note from the Author:

So many times, as described in these pages, I have felt hopeful. It seems that the more I am disappointed and the more I am let down, the more hopeful I become afterward. I don't know if this story will ever truly end. My battle with mental illness continues, and every day I get a little stronger. The entire ordeal reminds me of a quote, something my grandfather wrote out in calligraphy. It still hung on the wall in my grandmother's living room after he died. It read:

"It is not the critic who counts; not the man who points out how the strong man stumbles, or where the doer of deeds could have done them better. The credit belongs to the man who is actually in the arena, whose face is marred by dust and sweat and blood; who strives valiantly; who errs, who comes short again and again, because there is no effort without error and shortcoming; but who does actually strive to do the deeds; who knows great enthusiasms, the great devotions; who spends himself in a worthy cause; who at the best knows in the end the triumph of high achievement, and who at the worst, if he fails, at least fails while daring greatly, so that his place shall never be with those cold and timid souls who neither know victory nor defeat."

- Theodore Roosevelt

With hindsight, this story did not end up being written to attract Mei's attention. It was written as an apology and a confession, a declaration of freedom. It was written to tell Johanna that I am very sorry, to tell Levi the truth about our friendship and to let Mei know that my feelings for her may be nothing more than a delusion. I want to show Russ that his actions were an extension of the human condition, the universal suffering we all must endure. This story was written to be an asset to those who struggle daily with their own thoughts, with their addiction, their mistakes and with their obsessions. This was written for those who have no one to support them or understand them, for those who have had the odds stacked against them and for those who are ashamed of who they are. More importantly it was written to give the victims of violence, intimidation and discrimination a voice.

In these pages may you find strength and the courage to face down your own demons. I am not here to give you answers, to tell you that there is a better way, or that you can be cured. I only want to show you that when life floors you, you have to get up and keep fighting. Some might find this story disheartening, but if this connects with you on any level it gives me the motivation I need to keep going. I just want to encourage you to share your story. Don't let anyone make you feel embarrassed or ashamed of the things you have done, the places you have been or the people you have met. If we keep our history secret, if we do not learn from one another, these conflicts will continue to repeat themselves just as they have in this novel.

The most beautiful thing about humanity is that we have the power to transmute our pain into wisdom. The most tragic thing about humanity is that we are so unwilling to be hurt. Struggle through your pain, find your wisdom and move forward. Share your story. I know you can do it.

Acknowledgements

Thank you first and foremost to my mother for helping me edit my first draft and giving me the courage to move forward with publishing. I will never be able to repay the love, time and money spent on raising me and then getting me back on my feet (several times).

Thank you to all of my readers: Dad, Ron, Andy, Kate, John, Marc, Theresa K, Ed, David, Kevin, Jessica, Henna, Angela, Denise, Theresa H, Amélie, Kelley, Tabitha, DR, Mareta, Jenna, Amanda, Henna and anyone else I have forgotten. Special thanks to Shayna and Mark G for additional reading and help with editing.

Thank you to my content editor Polly Tuckett, who fought for my cause early on and made some fine contributions to the story with all of her grace, wit and charm.

Thank you to Cherie, Elizabeth, Suzanne, Morgan and the rest of the staff at Between the Lines Publishing. I couldn't have done it without you!

Thank you to Julie for the amazing artwork and to Cindy for connecting us.

Thank you to my wonderful girlfriend Pakou, who held me up during the final parts of the editing process when rereading the story and wondering what the public would think would aggravate my PTSD. Thank you for asking me if I am okay and distracting me when it felt as though the stress from publishing a book like this would cause me to relapse again. Your continued love and support means so much to me.

Thank you to my family. You are the best people.

Thank you to you, the reader, for allowing me to speak my personal truth. I am forever grateful. For those of you who have not yet been allowed to speak, I am here for you. I hope that someday you too will have acknowledgements of your own.

About the Author

N. Daniel currently resides in Downtown Minneapolis and works as a live-in caregiver for a quadriplegic individual. When he isn't writing or caring for his client you can find him wandering the city's skyways, music blasting in his headphones, or walking along the Mississippi river with family and friends. He frequently volunteers at outreach organizations in the Twin Cities community. His beliefs center strongly around charity, service to others and supporting causes that protect personal freedoms, especially for the disabled, the poor, those unfairly stigmatized by mental illness, and anyone who suffers. He is inspired by redemption stories, especially the character arc of Jean Valjean in Victor Hugo's Les Miserables.

Follow N. Daniel on Twitter @MyUnsafePlace or visit his blog at www.ndaniel.us

Artwork by Julie Ann Arenas, a dear friend living in Pasig, Philippines.

Sometimes it can be hard to talk to a loved one about mental illness.

If you are the friend or relative of someone struggling with their mental health and need advice on how to help, contact:

The National Alliance on Mental Illness (NAMI)
www.NAMI.org
HELPLINE: 1-800-950-NAMI (6264)
Email: info@nami.org

If you feel you are struggling or are having thoughts of hurting yourself or others, call:

National Suicide Prevention Lifeline
1-800-273-8255 - Available 24 Hours a Day

or visit your nearest emergency room.

Trust me, it will help.

Made in the USA
San Bernardino,
CA